AF323211

THE LIFE AND WORKS OF
RUSKIN BOND

Recent Titles in
Contributions to the Study of World Literature

Aristocracies of Fiction: The Idea of Aristocracy in Late-Nineteenth-Century and Early-Twentieth-Century Literary Culture
Len Platt

Salman Rushdie's Postcolonial Metaphors: Migration, Translation, Hybridity, Blasphemy, and Globalization
Jaina C. Sanga

Imagining Africa: Landscape in H. Rider Haggard's African Romances
Lindy Stiebel

Seduction and Death in Muriel Spark's Fiction
Fotini E. Apostolou

Unorthodox Views: Reflections on Reality, Truth, and Meaning in Current Social, Cultural, and Critical Discourse
James L. Battersby

Judgment and Justification in the Nineteenth-Century Novel of Adultery
Maria R. Rippon

The Late Modernism of Cormac McCarthy
David Holloway

The Colonial Conan Doyle: British Imperialism, Irish Nationalism, and the Gothic
Catherine Wynne

In My Own Shire: Region and Belonging in British Writing, 1840–1970
Stephen Wade

Multicultural Literature for Children and Young Adults: Reflections on Critical Issues
Mingshui Cai

Interfering Values in the Nineteenth-Century British Novel: Austen, Dickens, Eliot, Hardy, and the Ethics of Criticism
Jeffrey Moxham

Interactive Fictions: Scenes of Storytelling in the Novel
Yael Halevi-Wise

THE LIFE AND WORKS OF RUSKIN BOND

MEENA G. KHORANA

Contributions to the Study of World Literature, Number 121

Westport, Connecticut
London

Library of Congress Cataloging-in-Publication Data

Khorana, Meena.
The life and works of Ruskin Bond / Meena G. Khorana.
p. cm. — (Contributions to the study of world literature, ISSN 0738–9345 ; no. 121)
Includes bibliographical references and index.
ISBN 0–313–31185–4 (alk. paper)
1. Bond, Ruskin. 2. Authors, English—20th century—Biography. 3. British—India—Biography. 4. India—In literature. I. Title. II. Series.
PR6052.O57Z75 2003
823'.914—dc21 2002193032

British Library Cataloguing in Publication Data is available.

Library of Congress Catalog Card Number: 2002193032
ISBN: 0–313–31185–4
ISSN: 0738–9345

First published in 2003

Praeger Publishers, 88 Post Road West, Westport, CT 06881
An imprint of Greenwood Publishing Group, Inc.
www.praeger.com

Printed in the United States of America

The paper used in this book complies with the Permanent Paper Standard issued by the National Information Standards Organization (Z39.48–1984).

10 9 8 7 6 5 4 3 2 1

Copyright Acknowledgments

The author and publisher gratefully acknowledge permission to use materials from the following:

Ruskin Bond, selected passages or quotations from interviews, conversations, published works, and unpublished papers.

Diana Athill, comments from personal correspondence.

Johns Hopkins University Press, *The Lion and the Unicorn*, vol. 19, no. 2 (December 1995): Meena Khorana, "The River Is Eternal: Nature Mysticism and Vedanta Philosophy in Ruskin Bond's *Angry River*," pp. 253–68.

Cricket Magazine, selected comments about Ruskin Bond.

Scholastic India (Gurgaon), selected passages from poems by Ruskin Bond, in *Granny's Tree Climbing and Other Poems* (2000).

Pencraft Publications (New Delhi), *The Creative Contours of Ruskin Bond: An Anthology of Critical Writings,* Prabhat K. Singh, editor (1995): Meena Khorana, "The Search for an Identity: Journey as Metaphor in *The Room on the Roof,*" pp. 71–81.

Penguin Books India (New Delhi), selected passages from the following works by Ruskin Bond: *Delhi Is Not Far: The Best of Ruskin Bond* (1994), *A Flight of Pigeons: Collected Fiction* (1999), *The Lamp Is Lit: Leaves from a Journal* (1998), *The Night Train at Deoli* (1988), *Our Trees Still Grow in Dehra* (1991), *Panther's Moon and Other Stories* (1991), *Rain in the Mountains: Notes from the Himalayas* (1993), *The Room on the Roof* (1987), *Scenes from a Writer's Life: A Memoir* (1997), *Time Stops at Shamli and Other Stories* (1989), *The Room on the Roof and Vagrants in the Valley: Two Novels of Adolescence* (1993).

FOR MY DAUGHTER, ROHINI

Contents

Preface

I "discovered" the works of Ruskin Bond nearly sixteen years ago while working on my first book, *The Indian Subcontinent in Literature for Children and Young Adults: An Annotated Bibliography of English-Language Books* (Greenwood Press, 1991). I read more than a thousand books (in a variety of genres) for this project, but the only fictional work that captured the world of my childhood was Bond's *The Room on the Roof*, especially his description of the protagonist's bicycle ride on a hilly road with his friends. That scene reminded me of a ride that I had taken as a teenager down a steep mountainous road in Shimla—a strictly forbidden activity—and how my cycle kept going faster and faster, totally out of control, and then luckily it crashed against the side of the mountain instead of going down the mile-deep *khud* ("ravine"). Bond's strong evocation of the Himalayan setting also recalled happy memories of studying at a British public school in Shimla, Auckland House, the sister school of Bishop Cotton, where Bond had studied, and of summer vacations at my grandparents' homes in Shimla and Kashmir. This ability to project a vision of India that the reader can identify with is one of the most endearing characteristics of Bond's work. I was inspired to read everything by the author, and *The Life and Works of Ruskin Bond* is the outcome of that interest.

Ruskin Bond is a highly autobiographical author; hence, this critical analysis of his oeuvre has taken the form of a literary biography—that is, the book examines the impact of personal, historical, social, and literary influences on how his ideas were shaped and on the development of his career as an author. Chapter 1 places his life and works in the context of the end of British colonial rule in India and the postcolonial diaspora of the British from India. This chapter also provides an account of Bond's family in India, his personal experiences as a child and teenager, and, finally, his move to Jersey and London to pursue his dream of becoming an author. Subsequent chapters are structured according to the various stages of the author's life, mainly based on his place of residence, and the literary output associated with each phase. Chapter 2 focuses on Bond's years away from India and the acceptance of his first novel for publication. Chapters 3 and 4 describe his return to India and his struggle and determination to survive as an author under the difficult publishing circumstances in post-Independence India. Chapter 5 begins with Bond's move to Mussoorie in the foothills of the Himalayas, where he has settled permanently and from where he has been writing steadily for the past forty years. This chapter focuses on his short stories, novellas, and essays and the development of his canon for adults. Chapters 6 and 7 concentrate on his children's books and the growth of publishing for children in India. The last chapter evaluates Bond's long and still very productive writing career and summarizes his literary achievements and contribution to English writing in India for both adults and children.

In examining Bond's short stories, novellas, essays, and travel pieces, I have relied on the various collections in which they appear, instead of on the magazines or newspapers in which they were originally published. It is beyond the scope of this work to trace the long and interesting publishing history of each story or essay, some of them in newer incarnations. However, wherever pertinent, I have given a brief glimpse of the evolution of a significant short story or novella. I leave to some future researcher this time-consuming bibliographical task.

I have not taken any specific theoretical approach to the analysis of Bond's oeuvre; rather, each work has been examined on the basis of what influenced it, the literary genre, and the ideas and structures that emerge from it. Of special importance is the artistic use the author makes of his personal experiences and the impact of the Himalayan setting on his beliefs and worldview. I hope this book will also dispel the confusion surrounding the facts of the author's life and their transformation into fictional form.

In order to make these distinctions, I had to turn to the author on several occasions for clarification, and he graciously agreed to three personal interviews and many telephone conversations. I thank Ruskin for the patience and frankness with which he has answered my numerous questions—sometimes the same ones! Furthermore, the Ruskin Bond archives at the Mugar Memorial Library of Boston University proved to be a rich source of unpublished materials such as diaries, early drafts of books, and personal correspondence, as well as original documents such as birth certificates, the author's will, and family photographs. Frank and Malcolm Heppolette's ongoing research into the genealogy of the Bond, Clerke, and Heppolette families has revealed additional information about the author's ancestors in India. This unpublished material is now available at the Ruskin Bond archives.

Over the course of my research, I have received valuable assistance from many sources. I am grateful to Morgan State University for granting me sabbatical leave for the 1999–2000 academic year to work on this project. I thank Dr. Burney Hollis, dean of the College of Liberal Arts; Dr. Dolan Hubbard, chair of the Department of English and Language Arts; and my colleague Ms. Jewel Chambers for their continued support of my research. I have many family members in India to thank for their generosity, time, and active help toward this book: Vanita Saxena for arranging my trips to Mussoorie and for procuring copyright permissions from Bond's Indian publishers; Paritosh and Renu Gulati for interviewing Colonel Robindra Dewan at Bishop Cotton School, Shimla; Veena and Prem Varma for transcribing the audiotapes of my 1995 interview with Bond; and Rohit Gulati for making sure that each year I had copies of Bond's latest publications.

It has once again been a pleasure to publish with Greenwood Press—my fourth book with them—and I thank the senior editor, George Butler, for giving me the opportunity to work on this topic and the project editor, Katie Chase, for her professionalism and meticulous attention to detail in seeing the manuscript through each phase of production. I am deeply indebted to Susan Clawson for reviewing the manuscript and her willingness to discuss the organization of the individual chapters; to Lesli Lai for taking time from her very busy schedule to design and format the manuscript according to the publisher's guidelines; and to Jessie Rochford for her timely secretarial assistance. Finally, I thank my husband, Shami Khorana, and daughters, Shobna and Rohini, for their love and encouragement.

1

A Child of the British Raj

Ruskin Bond, a prominent Indian writer who lives in the Himalayan town of Mussoorie, is well known as a novelist, short story writer, poet, and essayist for children, young adults, and adults. An examination of Bond's life and work affords insight not only into his evolution as a writer but also into his contribution to the development of English literature in India and to the growing body of diasporic and postcolonial/post-Independence literatures.

Ruskin Bond is the author of six novels or novellas, over two hundred short stories, thirty-five books for children, four volumes of autobiography, 300–400 newspaper articles, five collections of essays, and four poetry collections. In addition, he continues to contribute articles regularly to leading newspapers and magazines in India and abroad. When Bond began publishing his stories in 1951, at the age of seventeen, Indian fiction in English had already begun to establish a tradition, beginning in the 1930s with the novels of Mulk Raj Anand, Raja Rao, and R. K. Narayan. These authors did not try to imitate the "King's English" or British orators and novelists; instead, they infused vitality, originality, and a distinctive Indian flavor into their prose. They were inspired by the rich oral traditions of their regions, Hindu mythology, and imagery from their natural surroundings to convey a truly Indian voice through the English language. English, which had been introduced by the British in the eighteenth century as the medium of instruction in higher education and as a language of scientific and scholarly communication, was no longer considered a foreign language by English-speaking Indians, even though most of them had another mother tongue. English also served as a common language among educated Indians from various parts of the country. According to Lakshmi Holstrom, "The writers of the 1930s were fortunate because after many years of use, English had become an Indian language used widely and at different levels of society, and therefore they could experiment more boldly and from a more secure position" (33).

When Bond arrived on the literary scene, he brought a more youthful, fresher voice to Indian writing in English. His works reflect both the influence of his Anglo-Indian[1] experiences and the impact of the changing political, social, and cultural conditions in India. Like Narayan, he has come to be known as a "regional" writer, who evokes the local color and atmosphere of the small towns and villages of the lower Himalayas. He brings a unique insider's perspective when describing the lives of simple rural or small-town people. Yet, his stories are also universal. Having lived through the colonial, postcolonial, and post-Independence phases of Indian life, and having traveled extensively in India, he is equally at ease with East and West, north Indian and south Indian, maharajahas and beggars, students and *tongawallahs* ("drivers of horse-drawn carriages"). He writes in the novella "Delhi Is Not Far": "Ours is a land of many people, many races; their diversity gives it colour and character. For all Indians to be alike would be as dull as for all sexes to be the same, for all human beings to be normal" (421). Through his thinly veiled autobiographical writings, Bond explores with sensitivity and imagination the experiences of his protagonists as they negotiate personal, national, and cultural boundaries.

Although Bond is the great-grandson, grandson, and son of Anglo-Indians, his work and attitude are surprisingly free from the prevalent colonial biases and stereotypes; rather, after decolonization he had the daring to reject his British nationality by embracing India, the land of his birth. In an essay entitled "On Being an Indian," he explains that his identity as an Indian is uncompromising: "Race did not make me one. Religion did not make me one. But history did. And in the long run, it's history that counts" (5).

Throughout India's 5,000-year-old history, all the major races, cultures, and religions of the world have made their contributions. Bond's personal history is very much a part of this multicultural fabric of India. The British East India Company was chartered in 1600 by Queen Elizabeth I to trade with the East Indies. In 1614 the Company appointed Sir Thomas Roe ambassador to the court of the Mughal emperor, Jehangir, and his mandate was to use diplomatic means to further trade with India. By 1623 the Dutch East India Company (founded in 1602) had taken control of trade in the East Indies, hence the British East India Company focused on India, setting up forts and trading centers on the eastern and western coasts of India—in Surat, Madras, Calcutta, and Bombay. The Company also faced a scramble for territory and trade from France and Portugal, the latter having colonized Goa, Daman, and Diu on the western coast since 1510. Under the able military leadership of Robert Clive, with his decisive victory in the Battle of Plassey in 1757, the British assumed power in Bengal, ousted France from India (with the exception of Pondicherry on the Coromandel coast), and strengthened the Company's administrative machinery in India. In the face of increasing British power in the subcontinent, the Dutch East India Company was dissolved in 1798. The British East India Company proceeded to extend its control (both territorial and trade) in India with the help of its vast army, which employed other Europeans as well as Indians (although only as common soldiers). After the 1857 Indian rebellion (called the "Indian Mutiny" by British historians) was crushed, the British Crown assumed political power in 1858 and set about colonizing India, referring to it as the "Jewel in the Crown."

Based on the 1931 census, just three years before Bond was born, there were 168,000 Europeans in India, of whom 60,000 were in the military, 12,000 in the civil service or government, and 21,000 in business or private occupations (Parry 31). Judging by these figures, the remaining 75,000 Europeans must have been women and children, mainly spouses or children of the above. British society in colonial India represented an island that cultivated isolation, racial superiority, and power. The British lived in the cantonments if they were in the military, or in the Civil Lines if they were part of the prestigious civil service. They saw no sense in belonging to India, because it was considered ill-mannered and inferior to "go native." This tiny "society of the exiles" (MacMillan 42) was bound together by a common culture and loneliness for family and friends in England. Brian Street writes, "[t]he white man felt that he was an alien in this strange land and that he could only survive by perpetuating his image of life in England, which recalled the seemingly trivial ritual, the tea parties, the balls, the dinners and the ceremonies" (31). They believed that it was by maintaining exclusivity from "natives" that they could uphold their position in India, and "any weakening of the team spirit would lead to a weakening of the Raj ["rule"] itself, and so they clung to each other with determination" (MacMillan 45). The anonymous author of an article entitled "The Romance of India," published in the July 1902 issue of *Quarterly Review*, advised:

> The English in India are wise to surround themselves, as far as they can, with English atmosphere, and to defend themselves from the magic of the land by sport, games, clubs and the chatter of fresh-imported girls, and by fairly regular attendance at Church. They are probably following the instincts of self-preservation; and certainly unless they remained themselves, they would not keep their Indian Empire. (Qtd. in Parry 53)

Margaret MacMillan, in *Women of the Raj*, writes that Anglo-Indian children were called the "outposts of Empire" (125), and that they "had their part to play, no matter how small, in the upholding of British prestige" (137). Their daily lives were strictly regimented with sports, play, lessons, socializing with British friends, and the rituals of eating, bathing, and sleeping in order to equip them for boarding school in England and for life as future colonial administrators.

The British community in India was elitist, strictly structured according to rank, wealth, family connections, and schooling. From the autobiographical writings of Rudyard Kipling, Rumer Godden, and M. M. Kaye, we learn of the lives of privileged colonial children during the Raj. In "Shrine of the 'Baba-Log'" Kipling writes: "I grew up in bright sunshine, I grew up with tremendous space, I grew up with animals, I grew up with excitement, I grew up believing that white people were superior" (21). Ironically, the aims of Empire were often subverted because Anglo-Indian children were products of a hybrid culture, taking from both their Indian and British experiences. Cultural barriers were generally bridged through servants, the only Indians British children knew intimately and came to love. Through their servants, the children were introduced to Indian languages, religious festivals, social customs, foods, and folktales. While *ayah*s ("nannies"), gardeners, gatekeepers, and cooks were employed to care for the daily needs of Anglo-Indian children, they were also friends who participated in the secret "illicit" adventures of their charges. Servants were indulgent and spoiled the children, and, according to MacMillan, parents were suspicious of the influence of servants during the formative years (128, 137–39).

Hence, after the age of five or six, the well-to-do sent their children "home" to England, because they believed that an English public school education (similar to a private boarding school in the United States) would enable their sons to compete for the civil service jobs in the colonies and their daughters for husbands in the colonial marriage market. Frequently, family members were separated for years at a time.

Pat Barr, in *The Dust in the Balance: British Women in India 1905–1945*, describes heart-rending scenes of parting as young boys and girls were sent to England to study (17–18). While parents blamed India for their sense of loss and disrupted family lives, the children missed their privileged childhood in India.

> They went from a world that was rich in colour and emotions to one that was cold and cramped. In India, they were spoiled and made much of; in Victorian and Edwardian England, they were thrust into a society where children were seen and not heard. They went to schools where India was to be driven out of their systems and Britain drummed in. (MacMillan 140)

For those who could not afford to send their children to England, there were many British schools in hill stations (resort towns) like Simla (now spelled Shimla), Mussoorie, and Darjeeling.

BOND'S EARLY CHILDHOOD

At the time of Ruskin Bond's birth in 1934, the political atmosphere in India had changed considerably in response to the urgent demands of the leaders of the Indian National Congress (established in 1885) and the Muslim League (1906) that England honor the 1919 Government of India Act, which provided for the transfer of power to elected Indian leaders. Upon returning to India in 1915, Mahatma Gandhi (1869–1948) had launched a nationwide Quit India movement that employed his principles of *Satyagraha*—passive resistance and noncooperation with British rule—techniques that he had successfully initiated in South Africa. On the diplomatic front, Mahatma Gandhi and other leaders were negotiating *Swaraj* ("self-rule") in London in a series of Round Table Conferences. By the 1930s, British administrators had realized that in the near future they would have to relinquish their Indian empire.

Bond is the third generation of his family in India on his father's side and the fourth generation on his mother's side.[2] His paternal grandfather, Herbert William Bond (b. 1863 in Islington, London), who was an apprentice to a London grocer, joined the Scottish Rifles as a foot soldier and came to India at the age of twenty. In 1894 he married Gloriana Elizabeth Enever (b. circa 1870), a German orphan who was brought up by Colonel Lesley on an indigo estate in Motihari, Bihar.

The couple had five children, all born in different cantonment towns in India because military personnel were transferred frequently: Herbert Henry (b. 1895), Aubrey Alexander (Ruskin's father; b. 1896), Arthur Cleveland (b. 1898), Gloriana Elizabeth (b. 1902), and Alma Eveline (b. 1903). Herbert William Bond settled in Calcutta after retiring from the army, and he died there at the age of fifty while his children were still young. Since theirs was an army family, the two oldest boys, Herbert Henry ("Uncle Bertie") and Ruskin's father, were sent to the Lawrence Royal Military School at Sanawar, a prestigious British public school in the Himalayan foothills that was also a military orphanage during that time. Uncle Bertie, who later worked as foreman in the Ishapur Rifle Factory, never married. Arthur, who also worked in the Ishapur factory, married twice; Gloriana died young; and Alma Eveline, who left India just before World War II, was killed in an air raid over Manchester. Upon finishing Senior Cambridge (high school), Aubrey began his teacher's training course in Sanawar (around 1916–17), the vocation that most suited his sensitive and scholarly personality. He then went to the equally well-known Lovedale School in Ootacamund (in the Nilgri hills in southern India) for a couple of years; it is unclear whether he went there to complete his training or to teach. Next, he worked as an assistant manager of a tea estate in Travancore, Cochin, before going back to teaching. He now started establishing schools for the royal children of small princely states on the Kathiawar coast in western India, such as Pithadia and Jamnagar. These schools, intended for up to ten or twelve children, were generally set up in the palace or on the palace grounds.

Bond's maternal grandfather, William Dudley Clerke, was born to Charles and Louisa Clerke in 1866 in Dera Ismail Khan (now in Pakistan), where Charles served as clerk in the commissioner's office. William Dudley worked for the Indian Railways and was one of the pioneers who helped bring the rail lines to Dehra Dun at the turn of the twentieth century (Bond, *Lamp* 99). The British had laid out an extensive railroad network in India, enabling them to transport raw materials to the seaports for shipment to factories in England and the finished products and consumer goods from England for sale on the Indian market. Today, thanks to the British, India has a very sophisticated railroad system—covering approximately 36,000 miles of track—which remains the primary mode of transportation for the majority of Indians. William Dudley had two daughters, Enid and Beryl, and a son, Kenneth Charles, by his first marriage; and after his wife's death, he married Ellen Catherine Sims in 1902, and they had three daughters—Emily Alice, Gwyneth "Gwen" Helena, and Edith Dorothy (Bond's mother).[3] Edith was born in 1913 in Karachi, now in Pakistan. She studied at Oak Grove for a few years, a school established by the Indian Railways in Jaripani (located between Dehra Dun and Mussoorie), but she completed her schooling at La Martiniere in Lucknow.

After retirement, William Dudley Clerke built a house at 6 Old Survey Road in Dehra Dun, the only one in Bond's family to own a house in India. Dehra (a local nickname for Dehra Dun), located in the Doon Valley below the Himalayan ranges, was favored by Anglo-Indians because of its pleasant climate, surrounding forests and orchards, and good hunting. Like nearly all the British-style bungalows built in Dehra by railroad officials, the house had a verandah all around it and a big walled compound, with a flower garden in front and a vegetable garden and orchard in the back. William Dudley died in Dehra in 1935, where he is buried. The family was not rich, but Ellen Clerke managed on the pension from the Indian Railways, sale of the fruit crops, and rent from letting out half the house to a Miss Kellner. Ruskin would visit this house often during school holidays, and it would later become the setting for several of his short stories and novellas. He says the "atmosphere [of Dehra] was to become a part of my mind and sensuous nature" ("Life" 147).

In 1933, Edith Clerke, who was enrolled in a nursing course at the Cottage Hospital in Mussoorie, met Aubrey Bond, who was on vacation after giving up his tea estate job. The couple married a few months later in Dehra when Edith was barely twenty and Aubrey nearly thirty-six (see *Rain* 60–61). Ruskin was born on May 19, 1934, in the military hospital in Kasauli, a hill station near Sanawar, where Aubrey had taken his pregnant wife for the delivery of their first child. Since the plains are very hot during the summer months, it was customary for well-to-do British and Indian families to go up to these resorts until the onset of the monsoons in June–July. In fact, all colonial offices would be moved each year to Simla, the summer capital of the Raj. Edith stayed with her sister Gwen Stevens and her husband, who was a doctor in Kasauli. Aubrey, who was now working for Alwar State, came to Kasauli to be with his wife at the time of Ruskin's birth. Ruskin was baptized in the Anglican church in Kasauli, and christened Owen Ruskin Bond. His father chose the name Ruskin after the famous Victorian author, because he appreciated the aesthetic, imaginative, and contemplative life.

A few months after Ruskin's birth, his father took a job in the princely state of Jamnagar as tutor-guardian to the royal children. Ruskin spent the first five years of his life in Jamnagar, where he was more exposed to Indian culture than the average British child in India. He grew up around the little princes and princesses, but he was equally comfortable with his Indian cook, ayah, and gardener, unconcerned with the barriers of caste or social station. Ruskin's sister, Edith Ellen, was born in Dehra in 1936, where his mother had gone for the baby's delivery. Ellen became ill with the polio virus and suffered brain damage and would remain handicapped and in need of care. In Jamnagar, Ruskin learned to read, and he developed a taste for comics and the classics of children's literature, which were read to him by his father. His favorite book was Lewis Carroll's *Alice's Adventures in Wonderland*, which gave him "a better appreciation of the absurdities of life" (*Scenes* 5). The young Ruskin's adventures in the palace grounds and in a deserted old palace had the same surreal charm for him as Alice's adventures. This was also an emotionally wrenching and insecure time for Ruskin, because his parents were not getting along. Perhaps Ellen's handicap may have added tension, disappointment, and responsibility to their lives.

In 1939 Bond's father, who was now past forty, left Jamnagar to join the Royal Air Force (RAF) as a pilot officer to help with the war effort. He was assigned to the cipher section at the headquarters in New Delhi. Joking about his last name and Agent 007, Bond writes: "So there was a Bond working in Intelligence long before the fictional James arrived on the scene" (*Scenes* 7). In the meantime, young Ruskin, along with his mother and baby sister Ellen, went to live with Grandmother Clerke in Dehra, because his father could not obtain married accommodations right away.

At the age of seven, he was sent by his mother to Hampton Court School in Mussoorie, where he spent a miserable year. Established in 1876–77 as a strictly nondenominational institution, the school was taken over by the Convent of Jesus and Mary nuns in 1912 (*Mussoorie and Landour* 45). The nuns were unsympathetic and strict, the food poor, the facilities inadequate, and punishments harsh (he was struck on the knuckles for not singing in tune). The only relief in this grim place were the letters he regularly received from his father, comforting him that books, toys, and stamps would be waiting for him when he returned. He tried running away from school with a friend, although they did not get very far. As a writer later on, this desire to escape from an oppressive situation would become a metaphor for seeking freedom and control over one's destiny.

Unexpectedly, his mother withdrew him from Hampton Court at the end of the academic term and put him (with the school party) on the night train to New Delhi. He was met by his father, and that is when he was informed that his parents had separated, although his father had tried several times to reconcile with his estranged wife. Ruskin would be in his father's custody, while Ellen would stay with their paternal grandmother, Gloriana Bond (who was in her seventies), in Calcutta. His brother, William, who was born in Dehra in 1942, would stay with his mother. He also learned that his mother was involved with a Punjabi businessman, Harbans Lal Hari, who owned a used car showroom and an auto repair shop in Dehra. Mr. Hari had left his wife because of the affair with Ruskin's mother.

Ruskin was to fictionalize these childhood experiences in the novella *Once upon a Monsoon Time* and the short story "The Room of Many Colours," which is actually the first half of the novella, covering the protagonist's life in Jamnagar. The story projects a Romantic or charmed view of childhood in which the protagonist (whose mother has left) is brought up in the loving, nurturing arms of his father, ayah, and gardener. There is a timelessness to the atmosphere of the palace and large garden, and the most ordinary activity is like a magical adventure to the young child. Even climbing up the spiral staircase to the mad Rani's ("queen's") tower to present her the nosegay made by the gardener is like a heroic adventure. His father informs him that she is actually a princess who went mad because of her frustrated love for a commoner, whom she was not allowed to marry; the child wonders if it is the gardener, Dukhi. While Father gives scientific and behavioral explanations to his many questions, Ayah always relies on a folktale or superstition. Thus, he always gets two different views on the same question. The Rani offers yet another perspective, the unconventional or the not "step-by-step" one. She brings discordant thinking, romance, fantasy, and wonder into his world—and just a hint of danger lurking beneath the surface. The young protagonist connects this fantasy to the reality of his daily life, and then tries to understand reality through the stories and explanations offered by his father, Ayah, and Dukhi. On one of his visits to the Rani, he discovers a room with many-colored glass windows; she tells him: "I can see a different world through each pane of glass" (*Once* 21). This room is symbolic of the different ways in which the father, Ayah, Dukhi, and the Rani present the world to the impressionable child—a world in which there is room for everyone's reality. He gains respect for different cultures and peoples, commoners and royalty, Christian and Hindu, upper-caste and untouchable; respect for people who do not adhere to social norms, whether it is the "mad" Rani or his father, who had the courage to reject the accepted notions of masculinity.

The story also gently captures the personal upheaval that is creeping into the young protagonist's life with talk of going to England, Hitler, and World War II. His father explains that they will have to leave because India is not their country, but the child protests that he was born in India and should be allowed to stay. Ayah gives him reality in her own way; she says the British cannot leave India because the king refuses to return the jewels on his crown to India. The secure fabric of his life is threatened when his father goes to New Delhi to interview with the RAF for a job. Now images of fear and violence enter his consciousness—jackals howling outside, a snake hissing, a mongoose making off with an egg from the poultry farm (reminiscent of Kipling's *Rikki Tikki Tavi*). He threatens to run away if he is separated from his ayah (an emotionally traumatic experience described in many colonial novels),[4] but his ayah, who does not want to desert her young charge, agrees to move to Dehra. The protagonist's life in Dehra with his grandmother, ayah, and a new friend, the tonga driver, is continued in the second half of *Once upon a Monsoon Time*.

Ruskin's love for his ayah is also fictionalized in the short story "My First Love," where Ayah is the mother figure who takes care of his physical needs, comforts him when he is afraid at night, entertains him with fairy tales of princes turning into snakes, and introduces him to the "forbidden delights from the bazaar" ("Life" 142). As in *Once upon a Monsoon Time*, the young protagonist of this story is hurled into a world of harsh realities when Ayah announces that she is getting married to the tongawallah. The story has many Dickensian features: the tonga ride is reminiscent of the marriage of Barkis and Peggoty in *David Copperfield* and, like the hero of this book, the protagonist's only friend is also his nanny. The parting with Ayah is difficult, but "when the tonga finally took her away, there was a dazzling smile on her sweet and gentle face—the face of the lover whom I was never to see again" (25).

His parents' marital troubles and his father's pain and loneliness had a lasting effect on the shy and sensitive Ruskin, an effect that has influenced his attitude toward life and his writing. He blamed his mother for deserting them, especially since his father suffered from frequent bouts of malaria, and some of this hurt and anger can be detected in his stories. It was much later, as an adult, that he came to understand his mother's point of view and needs—and the incompatible relationship of his parents. While Aubrey was serious—he liked to read, enjoyed music, and pursued stamp collecting as a hobby—Mr. Hari shared his mother's vivacious and fun-filled attitude toward life. They loved going to parties, dances, movies, and *shikar* ("hunting"). Dehra, with a population of only 40,000, was a lively wartime recreational center for British and American soldiers (*Scenes* 78). It offered good hunting, and night life in the form of cafés, bars, night clubs, and dance halls.

From 1942 to 1943 Ruskin lived with his father in the wartime Air Force hutment assigned to him, probably without official permission. Bond says this was the happiest time of his childhood because he was free from the dull routine of school. He kept himself busy all day with reading books, listening to music, playing, and examining his father's stamp and postcard collections. His father was a nurturing and devoted parent, providing security, love, and guidance to the young child. He taught Ruskin literature, math, geography, and political history through fun activities. They visited record shops, went to movies and restaurants, explored old tombs and historical monuments, and took long walks—in other words, his father introduced him to the artistic and contemplative life. He was also encouraged to keep a journal, which proved to be Bond's only training as a writer. At first the journal consisted of lists of singers, records, movies, and Hollywood trivia, but eventually it would give him the discipline of writing regularly and recording everything he observed and thought.

"ETON OF THE EAST"

After this glorious year in New Delhi, Ruskin's father convinced his son that he needed formal schooling and the company of children his own age. He took Ruskin to Simla to visit Bishop Cotton School (BCS), called the "Eton of the East," which was then—and still is today—a highly prestigious school with an impressive alumni. Dignitaries like Lord Mountbatten, Viceroy of India (1947) and Governor General of India (1947–48), were invited as chief guests to the school's Founder's Day ceremonies. Established in 1866 on the principles of Dr. Thomas Arnold, who became headmaster of Rugby in 1828, the school was named after G.E.L. Cotton, Bishop of Calcutta. Like its British counterparts, BCS taught Anglo-Indian boys patriotism to England, strict discipline, obedience to authority, and sacrifice for one's ideals—

gentlemanly qualities that would prepare students for the leadership of colonial society in India (see Reed 5–9; Gathorne-Hardy 70–78). As was typical of British public schools, BCS was also organized on the hierarchical structure of headmaster, teachers, and prefects. The entire student body was divided into four houses—Curzon, Lefroy, Rivaz, and Ibbetson—and stiff competition among the houses was encouraged in order to build "team spirit" and group loyalty.

Ruskin was admitted to BCS in 1943, at the age of nine, and was placed in Ibbetson House, named after the governor of undivided Punjab. At that time, the school had British teachers and 80 percent of the student body was European or Anglo-Indian. However, after Independence in 1947, the demographics were reversed: the Indian students gradually increased to 80 or 90 percent, while the remaining 10 or 20 percent were children of Anglo-Indians or Europeans who had stayed on in India (Interview). In keeping with public school tradition, Ruskin soon acquired a nickname, "Horsey," because of his singing voice.

Ruskin's father stayed in Simla for a couple of weeks to complete admission formalities. This was a very special time for Ruskin—they went to restaurants and book shops, took long walks, and visited places associated with Kipling lore. His father told him Kipling stories while taking rickshaw rides. Ruskin writes in "Kipling's Simla" that his father's "stories of phantom-rickshaws and enchanted forests…planted in me the seeds of my writing career" (87). His father came to Simla to be with Ruskin during the short breaks, but at the end of the term (the academic year in the hill stations was from March to November) Ruskin spent the three-month winter break in New Delhi.

When Ruskin returned to school in 1944, his father was transferred to Calcutta, where Aubrey moved in with his mother and Ellen at 14 Park Lane. Now his father was much too far away to visit Simla during breaks, but he wrote regularly, giving Ruskin weekly news of Calcutta, Grandmother Bond and Ellen, and his stamp and record collections. His last letter shows interest in Ruskin's school work, provides guidance on improving his writing style, and anticipates the holidays when Ruskin would visit Calcutta at the end of 1944. However, his father's health had weakened considerably due to malaria, and he died a few weeks after this letter arrived. Ruskin learned about his father's untimely death from one of the masters, and the headmaster, Mr. Priestley, took away all his father's letters (except the last one), so that he would learn to be tough, working on the public school ideology that feeling was bad form and that control of one's emotions led to the strengthening of character. Ruskin was only ten at the time. Mr. Priestley proved to be cruel and insensitive, because he never returned the letters, even when Ruskin approached him at the end of the school term. Although the RAF would pay for his education at BCS, he felt insecure about his future and where he would live. His father had not been rich; his most valuable possession had been his extensive stamp collection, which he had started to sell gradually in preparation for the move to England and for Ruskin's education there. Aubrey Bond had taken a practical approach to their future because he also needed to provide for his elderly mother, Ellen, and the baby William (who was with his ex-wife); all three would obviously remain in India. However, after his death, the stamp collection was nowhere to be found, and Ruskin was left with no inheritance. Being idealistic, he did not care for money: "My father taught me to write. That was inheritance enough" ("Last Time" 59).

No one arranged for Ruskin to attend his father's funeral, which made it difficult for him to reconcile with his loss: "There being no tangible evidence of my father's death, it was, for me, not a death but a vanishing...and [I] subconsciously expected him to turn up (as he often did, when I most needed him) and deliver me from an unpleasant situation" ("Coming Home" 44–45). Years later, Bond would vicariously confront his feelings at the loss of his father by writing "The Funeral." In this short story, he exposes the insensitivity of adults for deciding what is good for the orphan protagonist when his father dies—that is, not allowing him to attend the funeral. In order to say farewell, the young boy follows the funeral procession from a distance and witnesses the rituals in the cemetery from behind a wall. The story touchingly expresses the child's fear that his father will not be resurrected because he is buried deep in the earth ("How could anyone, even a Samson, push his way back to the surface again?" [13]). The protagonist finds consolation in the thought that perhaps his father would escape the grave by growing into a tree. Clearly, the author combines the Hindu belief in reincarnation and transmigration of the soul with the Christian concept of Judgment Day. As in *Once upon a Monsoon Time*, this story also conveys the author's rejection of his mother by stating that the protagonist (whose mother had also left to marry someone else) had forgotten his mother.

Like the young boy in the story, Ruskin continued to envision his father as his guardian angel and protector, and henceforth he tried to live life remembering what his father had taught him. In 2001, at the age of nearly sixty-seven, Bond finally brought closure to his father's death when he visited his father's grave at Bhowanipore Cemetery in

Calcutta (now Kolkata), where Flight Lieutenant Bond was buried by his mother, Gloriana Bond. Maya Banerjee, wife of Ruskin Bond's friend and neighbor, Victor Banerjee, was instrumental in locating the grave (see Mukherjee).

Ruskin now had to spend his winter breaks with his mother and stepfather in Dehra, and he resented it. When he went home for the first time after his father's death, no one came to meet him at the train station. After waiting for a long time, he took a tonga to his Grandmother Clerke's house, because he did not even know his mother's new address. Apparently, his mother had mixed up the dates, and she and his stepfather had gone for shikar, leaving his brother William and two half-brothers in the care of servants. No doubt, Mr. Hari had assumed the role of Mr. Murdstone (from *David Copperfield*) in the young Ruskin's imagination, although the author admits that his stepfather never said a harsh word or abused him in any way (Interview). Ruskin simply felt neglected and insecure. In the short story "Coming Home to Dehra" and the autobiographical *Scenes from a Writer's Life*, he poignantly describes this first winter vacation after his father's death (32–34). At a very young age, Ruskin had to deal with the divorce of his parents, the remarriage of his mother, and the death of his father in rapid succession. Ruskin blamed his mother for being irresponsible and resented his stepfather, because he did not have sufficient time or outlets to deal with his emotions.

His mother and Mr. Hari liked to enjoy themselves, and they spent money freely instead of paying the rent. When Mr. Hari's business failed in 1945, they were evicted, and the family ended up in Grandmother Clerke's house. Ruskin's insecurity was so acute that he wondered how he would look after his siblings if his mother and Mr. Hari died in a car accident. In spite of all their partying, the couple was cut off socially—she by the Anglo-Indian community for marrying an Indian, and he for his business failures and for marrying a Britisher. Hence Ruskin did not have access to any social connections from either community.

His mother and Mr. Hari had a difficult relationship at first. During the winter of 1945–46, after the failure of Mr. Hari's business for a second time, the couple were separated. From 1946 to 1947, his mother got a job as manager of Green's Hotel in Dehra, while Mr. Hari was once again living with his first wife, who owned a grocery store. Around 1948, his sister Ellen was brought to Dehra in the care of a nanny, because his Grandmother Bond was too old to raise a child.

Although the RAF sent an allowance for her upkeep, the situation must have placed further stress on the couple's marriage.

Ruskin coped with his changed family circumstances and the ensuing loneliness by turning to books—"[t]hey were the great escape," he writes in his autobiography; "reading was my true religion. It helped me to discover my soul" (*Scenes* xv, 67). He borrowed books from his grandmother's house and the Ideal Book Depot, the main bookstore in Dehra; at that time, bookstores also operated lending libraries. Another "escape" during holidays was going to the movies and visiting his grandmother and her tenant, Miss Kellner, who had been physically handicapped since childhood because of an accident. He played cards with Miss Kellner, listened to her stories, and ate the sumptuous goodies she served him. He also became friends with his grandmother's old gardener, Dukhi, who would become the prototype for all gardeners in his fiction.

Ruskin's stepfather sometimes took him on shikar trips, lasting two or three days, but Ruskin was rather bored because nothing exciting happened—there were no man-eaters. Also, he empathized with the animals due to the "unsporty" action of the hunters, who would often hunt at night, shooting the animal only after blinding it with the headlights of their jeep or car. The short story "A Week in the Jungle" is a satirical account of one such shikar trip when he discovered a bookshelf in the *dak bungalow* ("forest resthouse"), filled with books by Dickens, P. G. Wodehouse, the ghost stories of M. R. James, Emily Brontë, and Shakespeare. This was a real treat because, when the adults went out for their daily hunt, Ruskin would stay back to read. In "A Week in the Jungle," the twelve-year-old protagonist accompanies Uncle Henry and his friends on a shikar expedition into the Terai jungle in the Siwalik Hills. While the "manly" hunters employ villagers to beat the jungle with drums to force a tiger to come out, the "sissy" protagonist, who is reading a novel, sees a panther in the compound making off with a dog. When he tells the hunters of his experience, they think he either is too imaginative or is lying, because big game have evaded them, and all they "bag" are two wild fowl. In the introduction to *Ruskin Bond's Treasury of Stories for Children*, Bond writes that his stepfather was "a poor shot, so he cannot really be blamed for the absence of wildlife today; but he did his best to eliminate every creature that came within his sights" (xi).

At school, Ruskin was the student in charge of the library, so here also the library became his "retreat and [his] private academy" (*Scenes* 75). He read frantically—adventures, spy and murder mysteries, comics of Captain Marvel and Superman, and novels by Hugh Walpole, R. M. Ballantyne, and Dickens. He was especially influenced by the short stories of A. E. Coppard, H. E. Bates, and William Saroyan, because he found that the genre suited his temperament; "snatching at life and recording its impressions and sensations rather than trying to digest it whole" (*Scenes* 75). He aspired to be like the writer-hero of Walpole's *Fortitude* or Dickens's *David Copperfield*, with whose sad childhood he identified. At BCS, when he was thirteen, Ruskin had already written his first novel, entitled "Nine Months," in which he satirized some of the teachers and described events at school during the course of an academic year. The manuscript, which filled two school notebooks, was discovered by a teacher. It was confiscated, and Ruskin never saw it again.

In his eight years at BCS, Ruskin left quite a legacy. He was very popular, particularly with Indian students. Being a boarder helped him to get to know fellow Indians from different racial, cultural, and religious backgrounds. He also became a hero with his peers because of his mischievous streak. He was constantly playing pranks, answering back, and upsetting teachers—in short, he seemed to act out their inner desires, because they did not have the courage to rebel against authority. However, his popularity was mainly based on sports—he was goalkeeper for the school's football (soccer) and field hockey teams (for football in 1948, 1949, and 1950); and he helped the school win a resounding victory against their rival school in Sanawar, his father's old school. Although Ruskin was not good in science and math, his love of reading and his writing skills helped him to win several awards for Ibbetson House in debating, essay writing, and acting in school plays. Ruskin Bond's name is inscribed in the school's literary and academic Hall of Fame in various categories: Hailey Literature Prize in 1949 and 1950; Shakespeare Award in 1949; and the Anderson Essay Prize in 1948, 1949, and 1950, the only student in the history of the school to win this award for three consecutive years, according to Colonel Robindra "Wendy" Dewan, current bursar and an "old boy" of BCS.[5]

His last year at school, 1950, was full of trouble. Ruskin rebelled against authority, describing himself as an "angry young man, in revolt against rules, traditions, conventions, examinations, authority of any kind" (*Scenes* 75). When, as house captain, Ruskin complained about the poor quality of the food, he was publicly "dressed down" in front of the entire House, and he lost the house captaincy for a short period.[6] He was especially in revolt against Mr. Fisher, who became the new headmaster in 1949. Mr. Fisher and his wife were insensitive to the children, discouraging them, playing favorites, and verbally abusing them. (Because of these reasons and other scandals, he was fired in 1952.) Ruskin was sixteen that year and he blamed the British public school system for "set[ting] impossible standards for the boys—standards that the staff and administrators could not uphold" (*Scenes* 77). He disliked the public school philosophy that corporal punishment was essential in order to discipline students and maintain strict authority over them. He also felt that the emphasis on "school spirit" led to an elitist attitude, because only upper-class, affluent families could afford schools like Bishop Cotton.

Ruskin was not the only one who felt that life at a British public school was not in tune with the reality of life in India. Critics hold the "public schools responsible for the decline of the British Empire because they mass-produced snobbish students lacking in individuality, imagination, and original thought" (Khorana xvi). Authors like E. M. Forster, Graham Greene, and George Orwell demonstrate that "the public schools and their products played a large part in the decline of British power and prestige" and that "lack of brotherhood and inability to love, destroyed all chances of an honest relationship between the colonies and England" (Reed 168).

It is significant that an autobiographical author like Ruskin Bond has not set any of his stories at BCS. According to Bond: "There was nothing to hide. Worse, from the writer's point of view there was nothing to reveal" (*Scenes* 78). The one exception is the autobiographical story "The Playing Fields of Simla," where he describes his friendship with Azhar (called Omar in the story), a new boy from the frontier region of Peshawar, and their various escapades against authority.[7] Their "great escape" from the confinement of school was crawling through a dry tunnel (a drain for rain water) that led outside the school boundaries. They were kindred souls—quiet, lonely, and grieving over the deaths of their fathers—who shared their innermost thoughts, fears, and aspirations. Both were on the school's hockey team—Omar was fullback, while the narrator was goalkeeper—and when they won the match in Sanawar, they became heroes at school. But the story does not focus on life at BCS; rather, it is an account of their friendship against the background of the social and political chaos that was taking place in 1947. Ironically, Omar and the narrator ended up belonging to two different countries when India was partitioned into India and Pakistan. When communal riots broke out in Simla, Omar and fifty other Muslim students whose homes were now in Pakistan were escorted home from school by armed convoy. Omar reached Pakistan safely, but many years later, when India and Pakistan were at war, Omar's plane was shot down while on a bombing raid over the plains below Simla. The underlying questions posed by the story are whether national loyalties can shift so easily, and whether Omar thought of their friendship as he flew his bomber jet near Simla.

IN DEHRA, 1951

In December 1950, Ruskin returned to Dehra after completing his Senior Cambridge with a second division (equivalent to a B grade). Still resentful over his mother's marriage to Mr. Hari, he was reluctant to stay with his family; he yearned for privacy and freedom. He was so eager to express himself through his writing and to become a published author that he resolved that, like some of the great authors he had read, he did not need further formal education to be a writer. After a quarrel with his mother, he left home and spent a few days on train platforms and park benches. When he realized that he could not live like a vagrant, he returned home, announcing that he would stay only until he found a job. He was given a room on the roof of the old building in which they lived, which had its own entrance and a window from which he could gaze at the trees and the Himalayas.

He no longer had his Grandmother Clerke's house to go to because she had died in Ranchi on the eve of Indian Independence (on August 13, 1947), at the age of seventy-six, and the house had been inherited by his mother's eldest sister, Emily. Within a year, Aunt Emily, who was married to Dr. John Heppolette, a well-known South Indian Christian doctor, sold the house and left for Jersey in the Channel Islands. Bond's remaining aunts, all of whom were married and well settled, also moved out of India after Independence: one moved to England, one to New Zealand, and one to East Africa. Their only brother, the "eccentric" Uncle Ken, went to England. Uncle Bertie, his father's brother, would move to England in 1953 after the death of his mother, Gloriana Bond, in Calcutta. (Bond was to meet him in London in 1954.) Bond's mother was the only member of the family to remain in India. In the meantime, he was also thinking about his future and the possibility of going to England.

Bond spent most of 1951 wandering around Dehra, absorbing its flavor, observing trains, *dhobis* ("washermen"), and wrestlers, and playing football and cricket in the *maidan* ("open ground"). He made many Indian friends—Somi, Kishen, Daljeet, Haripal, and Ranbir and his sister Raj, to whom he was attracted—visiting their homes, playing badminton, and taking bicycle rides in the outlying areas of Dehra. He wore Indian clothes, ate Indian food, accompanied his friends to the Sikh and Hindu temples, and listened to the folktales and religious stories told by his friends' mothers.[8] On the hospitality of his friends and their families, he says: "I think they felt rather sorry for me, because I was so young. If anything, they blamed my mother and stepfather" (Interview). Having an Indian stepfather also brought Bond in touch with Indian families, providing him further access and insight into Indian culture. Much of this period of his life forms the raw material for his first novel, *The Room on the Roof.*

While he was nurturing his Indian heritage, his Anglo-Indian heritage was slipping away from him—quite literally. All middle-aged and young Anglo-Indians who had careers, relatives in England, property, or other connections had left India after Independence. (Once the colonial government was disbanded, there were few job prospects for the middle-aged in India, unless they were highly qualified.) But for the elderly and the middle-aged who were born and raised in India, the country was their only home—and they did not have the energy, or the desire, to start a new life elsewhere. Their stories speak of loneliness: they do not have many friends, except loyal servants; they are getting old and infirm and are often short of money because their pensions cannot keep up with inflation; and everyone they knew (their relatives and friends) has either left or died. Bond has written some touching portraits of Anglo-Indians who stayed on, such as Miss Kellner, Miss Ripley-Bean, and Mrs. Deeds. He writes: "They were the flotsam of Empire, jettisoned by the very people who brought them into existence" (*Scenes* 47).[9]

Even as a child, Bond had always enjoyed the company of older people, listening to their stories and experiences. When Miss Kellner died in 1951, he was the only young person to attend her funeral, which "was a funeral for everyone, because most of those present knew that it would not be long before they would be laid to rest beside her" (*Scenes* 88). Graveyards are an important subject and symbol of Anglo-Indian writing and life, because the inevitable end of those who had stayed on is death—symbolizing the end of the Raj, the end of an era.

Bond also started to write for publication in 1951. His journal entries not only reveal his thoughtful and sensitive personality, but they also indicate that he was developing a distinct style of writing—the ability to express deeply felt emotions with simplicity, touching descriptions of nature and people, a sense of humor, extreme honesty and self-analysis, and an amazing understanding of life for one so young. He would first submit a story to prestigious magazines like *The Illustrated Weekly of India* or *The Sunday Statesman*, but when it was rejected, he would send it to *My Magazine of India*, a small magazine published from Madras (now Chennai). His first published works were a couple of mystery stories that appeared in *My Magazine*, for which he received five rupees. He found that most editors lost interest in his writing when they learned that he was only seventeen, so he tried to give the impression through his writings that he was old. He finally published a story, "My Call," a humorous piece about a school master at BCS, in *Illustrated Weekly* in August 1951, just before leaving for Jersey, for which he received Rs 50, the going rate for established writers.[10]

His grandmother, Ellen Clerke, who had always been worried about Ruskin's future, especially because of Mr. Hari's declining business, had taken out an insurance policy in his name. The policy matured in 1951, and the money was sufficient to pay for his passage to Jersey. At his mother's request, Aunt Emily agreed to let Ruskin move in with her family in Jersey until he could support himself. Ruskin was now ready to take on the world and to fulfill his dream of becoming a writer. From Aunt Emily's house he would be close to the literary world of London, where he had hopes of publishing his books. However, his decision also led to inner conflict. One journal entry about leaving India states, "Perhaps I am rotting here, perhaps the West will do me good. I have achieved nothing. I have achieved nothing but happiness" (*Scenes* 114). He tries to analyze his motives for giving up this happiness to enter a world of "rush and work and worry": "it is the desire for recognition and applause that lures me away. I tell myself that fame is not greatness, and that if I remain as I am long enough I shall soon grow accustomed to obscurity. At least I shall retain my individuality, and in art that is most important" (*Scenes* 114, 121). His dilemma of whether to be loyal to India and his friends in Dehra or to pursue his dream abroad embodies what Homi Bhabha states is the "sense of the nation as one of the major structures of ideological ambivalence within the cultural representations of 'modernity'" (4).

On October 14, 1951, at the age of seventeen, Bond left Dehra by train, leaving the safety of home and the comfort of friends to go alone to a new country. The last entry in his Dehra journal is a farewell to India and his childhood: "For once I realized how young I was, how old I had tried to be and thought I was, and for once I appreciated my youth" (*Scenes* 127). And he is determined never to lose sight of his joyous youth in India:

> To love and be loved is the greatest happiness....Men and women leave the age of childhood behind, and are so busy with their buyings and sellings, their ambitions and their hopes, their loves and their hates, that they forget they once lived in a land where dreams were real. I will not forget my childhood, I shall not surrender it. (*Scenes* 130)

NOTES

1. Throughout this book, the word Anglo-Indian is used in its original sense to mean the British in India, and not its later official definition to describe people of mixed Indian and British descent. In the novella "A Handful of Nuts," Bond has the following to say about the term: "The expression, 'Anglo-Indian,' has come to mean so many things—British settler, old *Koi-Hai*, Colonel Curry or Captain Chappati, or simply Eurasian—that I don't use it very often. Indian is good enough for me" (48).

2. Unless indicated otherwise, the biographical information is based on my extensive interviews and telephone conversations with Ruskin Bond, and on the first volume of his autobiography, *Scenes from a Writer's Life: A Memoir*, which focuses on defining events rather than on presenting a chronological narration of his life.

3. According to a family tree compiled by Frank and Malcolm Heppolette (related to Emily and John Heppolette, Bond's aunt and uncle in Jersey), William Dudley Clerke had a second son, Arnold Basil (b. 1893), by his first wife (Alice Nora Bailey). This unpublished research was conducted in 2000 at the India Office Collections in the British Library in London.

4. See Iris Macfarlane's *The Children of Bird God Hill.*

5. Colonel Dewan (in BCS: 1947–54) was two or three years junior to Ruskin Bond. The "Old Boy" network, called the Old Cottonian Association, still meets once a year at the Cumberland Hotel, near Oxford Street, London. Colonel Dewan attended a reunion in 1995; Gay Niblett is the current chairman of the organization.

6. Bond was captain of Ibbetson House in 1949 and 1950. He was succeeded by Virbhadra Singh, who would later become the chief minister of the state of Himachal Pradesh in the 1980s and 1990s.

7. In early 2002, Bond announced that he would honor the school's request that he assist in writing the history of Bishop Cotton School. The school will send all the necessary research materials to Mussoorie, and Bond will serve as consulting editor and write the introduction to the book.

8. For a discussion of the forces of "consent" and "descent" as related to the construction of ethnicity and race, see Werner Sollors's *Beyond Ethnicity* and *The Invention of Ethnicity.*

9. Also see Paul Scott's novel, *Staying On.*
10. Bond has no copies of these early stories (Interview).

WORKS CITED

Barr, Pat. *The Dust in the Balance: British Women in India 1905–1945.* London: Hamish Hamilton, 1989.

Bhabha, Homi K. "Introduction: Narrating the Nation." *Nation and Narration.* Ed. Bhabha. London and New York: Routledge, 1990. 1–7.

Bond, Ruskin. "Coming Home to Dehra." Bond, *Our Trees* 39–45.

___. "Delhi Is Not Far." Bond, *Delhi Is Not Far* 353–428.

___. *Delhi Is Not Far: The Best of Ruskin Bond.* New Delhi: Penguin, 1994.

___. "The Funeral." Bond, *Time Stops* 11–14.

___. "A Handful of Nuts." *Strangers in the Night: Two Novellas.* New Delhi: Penguin, 1996. 1–80.

___. Interview with Meena Khorana. Mussoorie, July 1995.

___. "Kipling's Simla." *Strange Men, Strange Places.* By Bond. New Delhi: Rupa, 1992. 85–90.

___. *The Lamp Is Lit: Leaves from a Journal.* New Delhi: Penguin, 1998.

___. "The Last Time I Saw Delhi." Bond, *Our Trees* 63–66.

___. "Life at My Own Pace." Bond, *Delhi Is Not Far* 141–50.

___. *Mussoorie and Landour: Days of Wine and Roses.* New Delhi: Lustre, 1992.

___. "My First Love." Bond, *Delhi Is Not Far* 21–25.

___. "On Being an Indian." *A Garland of Memories.* By Bond. New Delhi: Mukul Prakashan, 1982. 4–5.

___. *Once upon a Monsoon Time.* Hyderabad: Orient Longman, 1974.

___. *Our Trees Still Grow in Dehra.* New Delhi: Penguin, 1991.

___. "The Playing Fields of Simla." Bond, *Scenes* 51–59.

___. *Rain in the Mountains: Notes from the Himalayas.* New Delhi: Viking/ Penguin, 1993.

___. "The Room of Many Colours." Bond, *Time Stops* 15–34.

___. *The Room on the Roof.* London: André Deutsch, 1956.

___. *Ruskin Bond's Treasury of Stories for Children.* New Delhi: Viking, 2000.

___. *Scenes from a Writer's Life: A Memoir.* New Delhi: Penguin, 1997.

___. *Time Stops at Shamli and Other Stories.* New Delhi: Penguin, 1989.

___. "A Week in the Jungle." *Grandfather's Private Zoo.* By Bond. Bombay: India Book House, 1967. 71–80.

Dewan, Robindra. Interview with Paritosh and Renu Gulati. Shimla, 12 August 1995.

Gathorne-Hardy, Jonathan. *The Old School Tie: The Phenomenon of the English Public School.* New York: Viking, 1978.

Holstrom, Lakshmi. *The Novels of R. K. Narayan.* Calcutta: Writers Workshop, 1973.

Khorana, Meena. Introduction. *British Children's Writers 1800–1880*. Ed. Khorana. Dictionary of Literary Biography 163. Detroit: Gale Research, 1996. Xi–xx.

Kipling, Rudyard. "Shrine of the 'Baba-Log.'" *Plain Tales from the Hills: Images of British India in the Twentieth Century*. Ed. Charles Allen. London: André Deutsch and British Broadcasting Corporation, 1975.

Macfarlane, Iris. *The Children of Bird God Hill*. New York: McGraw-Hill, 1967.

MacMillan, Margaret. *Women of the Raj*. New York: Thames and Hudson, 1988.

Mukherjee, Susmita. "Ruskin Bonds with Dad in Kolkata." *The Telegraph* [Kolkata], 23 Jan. 2001.

Parry, Benita. *Delusions and Discoveries: Studies on India in the British Imagination 1880–1930*. Berkeley and Los Angeles: U of California P, 1972.

Reed, John R. *Old School Ties: The Public Schools in British Literature*. Syracuse: Syracuse UP, 1964.

Scott, Paul. *Staying On*. New York: Morrow, 1977.

Sollors, Werner. *Beyond Ethnicity*. Oxford: Oxford UP, 1986.

___. *The Invention of Ethnicity*. Oxford: Oxford UP, 1989.

Street, Brian V. *The Savage in Literature: Representations of "Primitive" Society in English Fiction 1858–1920*. London and Boston: Routledge, 1975.

2

At "Home" in England? A Postcolonial Dilemma

In November 1951, seventeen-year-old Ruskin Bond sailed alone from Bombay's Ballard Pier, aboard the P & O liner *Strathnaver*, for Jersey in the Channel Islands. His journey can be seen as the quest of an archetypal hero whose courage and determination would enable him to resolve his identity crisis and to pursue his ambition of becoming a published author.

The small island of Jersey, which is fourteen miles from the French coast, was occupied by German forces during World War II. After liberation in 1945, it became self-governing, but the United Kingdom continued its 900-year-old relationship with the island by maintaining responsibility for its defense ("States"). When Bond arrived at his Aunt Emily's home in Jersey, he had only three or four pounds left from his travel money. Since he did not want to be a burden on his relatives, he looked for a job in St. Helier, the capital and port of Jersey. It was easy to find employment in those days, and he held three jobs at various times, including assistant to the Thomas Cook travel agent in Jersey and wages clerk in the Public Health Department, where he earned £4 per week. He also took the Jersey Civil Service examination and was placed fourth in order of merit. Although he was offered a post in the Civil Service, he could not envision spending the rest of his life on a cold island with a 45-square-mile area, despite its reputation as "the sunniest spot" in the British Isles. Moreover, the holiday resort atmosphere of Jersey did not suit his temperament.[1]

In Jersey, Bond was terribly homesick for India. The irony of his situation was that in India he was a foreigner because of his race and British parentage; yet, when he came "home" to Jersey, he was not only in a place that was foreign to him but where he was regarded as an outsider because he was Anglo-Indian. This sense of deracination, of not belonging anywhere, was a dilemma experienced by many colonial children. Their confusion and loss have been poignantly described in many fictional and autobiographical works in which British children are separated from parents and home in India to study at public schools in England—such as in Jon and Rumer Godden's *Two under the Indian Sun* and M. M. Kaye's *The Sun in the Morning*. To the protagonists, India represented the lost world of their "golden" childhoods, of indulgence and unconditional love from servants, of sunshine and freedom. Ruskin Bond, far from "recovering" his English identity after moving to Jersey and later to London, resolved his inner conflicts and affirmed his identity as an Indian. His autobiography, *Scenes from a Writer's Life*, reveals his longing for the familiar images and atmosphere of India:

> ...even though my forefathers were British, Britain was not really my place. I did not belong to the bright lights of Piccadilly and Leicester Square; or, for that matter, to the apple orchards of Kent or the strawberry fields of Berkshire. I belonged, very firmly, to peepal trees and mango groves; to sleepy little towns all over India; to hot sunshine, muddy canals, the pungent smell of marigolds; the hills of home; spicy odours, wet earth after summer rain, neem pods bursting; laughing brown faces; and the intimacy of human contact. (154–55)

Bond's sense of dislocation was further intensified because he did not get along particularly well with his aunt, uncle, and cousins. They constantly criticized him for being *too* Indian—for his Indian accent, regular correspondence with friends in Dehra, and love for India. He told me in his home in Mussoorie that even though his aunt was Anglo-Indian and his uncle a South Indian doctor, they maintained an anti-Indian attitude, perhaps because they had to leave India or because they felt that the Raj days were better (Interview). He describes his relatives as "champions of Empire" who wanted him to forget his ties with India and "be more British in my preferences and attitudes" (*Scenes* 142, 143). Ruskin wanted desperately to "return to the sensuous welcoming arms of the land [he] had left" (*Lamp* xiii), but he had neither the money for the return passage nor prospects of a steady income in India.

In the meantime, Bond captured his longing for India by writing short stories set in Dehra and regularly submitting his work to the *Illustrated Weekly* in India. In 1952 the magazine published "Untouchable," written when he was sixteen and submitted for publication while he was still in India. It is his first published story to have survived. "Maharani," a story about a cow in a Dehra bazaar, was published in 1954. The character Kishen, who would feature prominently in Bond's first two novels, was first introduced in this short story.

Jean Renoir's newly released color film *The River*, based on Rumer Godden's autobiographical novel by the same title, poignantly reflected Bond's sentiments for India. The movie ran for a couple of weeks in St. Helier in 1952, and Bond went to see it several times because everything Indian appealed to him. He had read the novel, but it was the movie that captivated him with its lyrical representation of the English family living on the banks of a river, and by the efforts of the children to liberate themselves from the "colonial compartmentalization" (M. Harris 20) of their lives in British India. The tropes in the novel do not focus on barriers but on crossing them: the road to their house goes through the bazaar and the smells and sounds of India reach them all day—and they are fascinated by them. In the heat of the afternoon sun or at night, when the *sahibs* ("gentlemen") and servants are asleep, the children venture forth into the enchantment of India—to explore, to play fantasy games, and to have meaningful experiences in the land of their birth.

The movie not only struck a responsive chord in Bond, but it prompted him to begin writing his intensely autobiographical first novel, *The Room on the Roof*, in order to recall the "people and places [he] had known and loved" in India ("Typewriter" 110). Like his role model David Copperfield, Ruskin worked diligently at his job during the day, but spent the evenings in his attic room, shaping the journal entries he had made in 1951 into a first-person account of his friends and experiences in Dehra. Working on this novel took Bond vicariously to the places he missed, and no doubt helped to resolve his cultural confusion and ambiguity.

> I was only seventeen. But out of my loneliness I produced a novel, raw, naïve and imperfect, but brimming with life and joy and truth, my own truth, for to be true to oneself is to be true to others. (*Lamp* xiii)

Mr. Bromley, a senior clerk in the Public Health Department, was so impressed by the dedication of the young author that he loaned him money to buy a typewriter, so that he could send a presentable manuscript to publishers. By the end of 1952, Bond had already submitted the manuscript to three publishers in London, and one of them, the newly founded André Deutsch publishing house, liked the novel but suggested he visit London in order to discuss changes (see "Typewriter"). On one of his lonely walks along the seafront, Bond "resolved that [he] was going to be a writer, come hell or high water, and that in order to do so [he] would have to leave Jersey and live and work in London" (*Scenes* 142). This resolve was fueled by a quarrel with his uncle over a diary entry in which Bond expressed his resentment of the colonial attitudes of his relatives. After spending eighteen months in Jersey, he left for London with the £12 he had saved from his salary.

For the first time in his life, Bond was completely on his own, an experience that gave him both freedom and self-confidence. In London he worked at a regular 9–5 job at Photax Ltd., a small company (on Charlotte Street off Tottenham Court Road) that manufactured photographic equipment, and he learned to survive on his meager salary of £6 per week. Although shy and reserved at first, he soon became popular with his colleagues because of his youth and because he kept them entertained with stories and a mischievous sense of humor, a quality that is reflected in his prose style and conversation.

Bond enjoyed living in London and felt at home in its cosmopolitan atmosphere. London offered him opportunities to indulge his artistic tendencies and love of reading: he went to the theater, movies, art galleries, book shops, and music and dance recitals. In addition, he made contacts with the British Broadcasting Corporation and gave short talks on its Home Service program on such topics as "My Two Homes" and "Spring Festival." He also made friends with many Indian students and attended their cultural events, but far from leading an insular life with Indians only, he made friends with students from Vietnam, Thailand, and Europe as well. Among his many friends was a Vietnamese woman, Vu-Phuong, to whom he proposed marriage, but she left London suddenly to visit her parents in Vietnam, because they had not contacted her since the beginning of the civil war between the North and South. He never heard from her again, but he has treasured the memory of that unrequited love.

In the midst of this busy life, Bond never lost sight of his goal of becoming a published author and returning to India. London had given him access to the publishing world, and he was especially fortunate that

Diana Athill, editor and junior partner at André Deutsch, had taken a personal interest in his career and in publishing *The Room on the Roof*.[2] Although nearly fifty years have passed since that time, Athill vividly recalls what attracted her to the book.

> What made me want us to publish him was simply the book itself....[I] was struck by how totally free his writing was of the kind of fault often apparent in the writing of young and unsophisticated people driven by a longing to be a writer. So often they feel it necessary to strive for a sophisticated effect, instead of trusting their own voices. But this boy had the innate good judgement to write about what he really knew, *in his own voice*. And the result, of course, was a freshness and authenticity which was charming as well as genuinely interesting.

Once she met him and learned of his personal circumstances, she "loved the book even more":

> He was such a brave little figure!...I do remember thinking that never *never* would I have had the courage to launch myself across the world like that, or the steadiness to then plod on in the dreary job he found, so sensibly and uncomplainingly. For such a young person he had an amazing amount of dignity, of an utterly unpretentious kind.

On Athill's editorial advice, Bond restructured the book from a first-person journal format to a fictional narrative in the third person. The eager young author was open to suggestions, and after two more drafts, the novel was accepted for publication. André Deutsch, of course, had taken a gamble in publishing the book, "a gamble that didn't come off," according to Athill, because it was not a financial success. Yet "the book was short, so it was not expensive to produce, which made the gamble a little one. Certainly the knowledge that it led Ruskin on to the kind of writing natural to him, and to *success* in that kind of writing, has been an ample reward as far as I am concerned" (Athill).

THE ROOM ON THE ROOF: A VICARIOUS SEARCH FOR "HOME"

The Room on the Roof is a complex novel that functions at several levels of experience and meaning simultaneously.[3] Apart from its obvious autobiographical elements, *The Room on the Roof* can be considered a pioneering young adult novel, even though young adult literature was not recognized as a literary genre at that time. Not surprisingly, when it was first published in 1956, the dust jacket described it as "an adult novel written by a teenager." The 1993 Penguin (India) edition more accurately defines it as a "novel of adolescence." According to Judith Rich Harris and Robert M. Liebert, "Adolescence is the transitional period from the dependency of childhood to the independence and responsibility of being an adult. At this point in their lives, young people struggle with two fundamental problems: to redefine their relationships with parents and other adults, and to establish themselves as individuals" (460). *The Room on the Roof* is a coming-of-age novel that explores the typically adolescent concerns of identity formation, alienation, rebellion against adult restrictions, personal autonomy, emerging sexuality, and financial independence. These themes and experiences—which the young author was undergoing while writing the novel—are presented with depth and feeling through the story of Rusty, an Anglo-Indian youth.

Set soon after Indian Independence, *The Room on the Roof* attacks the prevailing racial and colonial attitudes of the British through the existential anguish of seventeen-year-old Rusty and his search for identity and "place" in the new India. Like the author, Rusty is born in a hill station in the foothills of the Himalayas. Orphaned as a young child, Rusty is brought up as a *pukka* ("proper") British sahib by his guardian, Mr. Harrison. He studies in expensive British-style public schools in India and lives in the isolated European section of Dehra. There is a purposeful apartheid in the physical setting and construction of Anglo-Indian residences, which separated them from the mainstream of India. As Benita Parry has stated in *Delusions and Discoveries*, the colonials lived like exiles who were being threatened by the surrounding India (123), and they set up barriers between their British world and India.

> Mr. John Harrison's house, and the other houses, were all built in an English style, with neat front gardens and name-plates on the gates. The surroundings on the whole were so English that the people often found it difficult to believe that they did live at the foot of the Himalayas, surrounded by India's thickest jungles. *India started a mile away, where the bazaar began.* (My italics; *Room* 9)

Mr. Harrison, a stern and insensitive man, tries to inculcate a sense of racial superiority and exclusivity in Rusty—even though India is no longer a colony of the United Kingdom. Like so many others, he stays on after Independence either because of business interests or because he is used to the comforts that India can offer.

Rusty is a shy and withdrawn boy who feels disconnected from his surroundings: he has no friends, British or Indian, and his only contact with Indians is through the untouchable sweeper boy. The real world beyond the Clock Tower—the "bazaar and India and life itself" (14)—are forbidden to him. He finds relief and escape from his confined Anglo-Indian world through dreams of "sudden and perfect companionship, romance and heroics" (10). At the beginning of the story, Rusty operates within the narrow sphere of the European residential community, a world of privilege and convenience that is not rooted in the soil of India. He is "ready to do as his guardian wished: he had always obeyed him" (8), but he expresses his loneliness by wandering aimlessly in the hills, with his head drooping. At this point in his life, according to the theory of developmental psychologist James Marcia, Rusty's identity formation is fixed at the "foreclosure status," when the identity crisis is not faced because of his psychological dependency on his guardian; and at the "diffusion status," because he displays a lack of commitment and a general withdrawal from life (qtd. in Harris and Liebert 500).

Conflict is introduced into the plot when Rusty, on one of his solitary walks, strays away from the European section of Dehra and is offered a bicycle ride by a Sikh teenager, Somi. The easy friendship of Somi and his friends becomes a tempting invitation to cross the forbidden barrier into the Indian section of town. Rusty is, for the first time, confronted not only with challenging the authority of his guardian but also the unwritten law of colonials not to mix with "natives." Rusty is attracted to the warmth, hospitality, and disarming charm of Somi and his friends, and he recognizes his Anglo-Indian world for what it is—elitist, cruel, cold, and deprived.

Poised at a turning point in his life, Rusty is ready for a dynamic confrontation with Indian culture. As the hero of an archetypal journey would do, Rusty responds to the "call to adventure" and crosses into forbidden realms, where he faces many challenges on the road to adulthood and independence. He listens to the "devil in his heart" (11) and ventures past the Clock Tower into the bazaar, the place that British children had always been warned to stay away from. Rusty's rebellion, in Jungian terms, typifies the individual "who is endeavoring to discover and assert his personality" (Henderson 110). The noise and confusion, tastes and smells, beauty and squalor, and feverish activity of the bazaar represent a microcosm of the world to Rusty. It is like entering a mysterious, timeless place—significantly, there is no clock in the tower to mark the passage of time.

> ...the road was hot and close, alive with the cries of vendors and the smell of cattle and ripening dung. Children played hopscotch in alleyways or gambled with coins...cows moved leisurely through the crowd....And above the uneven tempo of the noise came the blare of a loudspeaker playing a popular piece of music.
>
> Rusty moved along with the crowd, fascinated by the sight of beggars lying on the roadside; naked and emaciated half-humans, some skeletons, some covered with sores; old men dying, children dying, mothers with sucking babies, living and dying. (14)

When Rusty returns home after secretly meeting his Indian friends in the bazaar, he is scolded for disobedience and caned mercilessly by his guardian: "You belong here, to this house, this road, these people. Don't go where you don't belong" (24). Yet Rusty continues to defy these rigid social codes because he is ready to move out of his narrow world into the vaster world that lies beyond—mysterious, forbidden, tempting. With this clash of his two worlds, Rusty has entered what Marcia calls the "moratorium status" in the ongoing identity crisis of adolescents, leading to frequent conflicts with authority figures (qtd. in Harris and Liebert 502).

Rusty's initiation into the Indian world is marked by his participation in Holi, the Hindu spring festival, which signifies the regeneration of the earth, awakening of love among people, and wiping away of social distinctions. People abandon social decorum by recklessly throwing colored powder on each other and singing and dancing to forget their problems and enmities. All of creation seems to rejoice in this promise of a new life: "The infection of spring spread simultaneously through the world of man and the world of nature, and made them one" (29). Rusty is happy for the first time in his life and he releases his pent-up emotions by responding to the excitement of Holi; it was "something wild and emotional, something that belonged to his dream-world" (28). He is greeted as an equal by his friends, and all racial and cultural distinctions disappear: "Gently, they rubbed [colored] dust on the boy's cheeks, and embraced him; they were like so many flaming demons that Rusty could not distinguish one from the other" (30). The celebrations not only connect him to the surroundings and people of India but also to the inner world of his dreams and fantasies.

> He wanted this to go on for ever, this day of feverish emotion, this life in another world. He did not want to leave the forest; it was safe, its earth soothed him, gathered him in, so that the pain of his body became a pleasure....
> *He did not want to go home.* (My italics; 32)

By participating in the rituals of an Indian festival, Rusty has crossed into that forbidden realm of India that most colonials denounced as primitive, licentious, evil, and exotic. Rusty, like the author, has not had any contact with Indian religions—not even in school after Independence—until his friends invite him to join them. When Rusty returns home, he is again beaten for ignoring what his guardian calls the difference between proper and improper, civilized and barbaric, decent and shameful. Mr. Harrison taunts him with being a "mongrel," half-English, half-Indian—a fact that had been hidden from Rusty—and for disregarding his upbringing and education as an Englishman. When Mr. Harrison compares him to the untouchable sweeper boy, Rusty defiantly claims to be just as good as the servant and just as good as any full-blooded Englishman. The festival of Holi has taught him to overcome class and caste distinctions, and he is not ashamed of his mixed racial heritage: "I'm as good as you! I'm as good as anyone!" (35). Although "[m]adness and freedom and violence were new to him" (40), Rusty repulses the attack of his guardian, beats him, and runs away from his rootless and stifling Anglo-Indian world to the pulsating life of India. This act of "crossing the threshold" symbolizes his psychological need to empower himself, and his readiness to take responsibility for his life and actions. He returns to the bazaar, the very womb of life, and is born anew.

Rusty's actions challenge the myth that a person's identity and sense of home are determined by racial and national ancestry alone. His journey away from his British world serves as an introduction to his Indian self and helps to formulate his personal ideals and the strength of character he will later need to stand by his choices. In addition, it extends his experiences to include peer group relationships, receiving and giving unconditional love, and a sense of family and security. Somi takes him home, and now Rusty dresses, eats, and lives as an Indian. When Rusty wants to become financially independent, Somi finds him a job teaching English to Kishen Kapoor, a spoiled only child, in exchange for room and board. For the first time in his life, Rusty gets what he desires most—a room of his own, his freedom, his place in the sun (see "What's Your Dream?"), and he dreams of becoming a writer. Enveloped in the comfort of belonging to a family, Rusty is amazed at how his Indian friends accept him so readily, even though he is a stranger to them.

The essential function of Rusty's journey of discovery "is the development of the individual's ego-consciousness—his awareness of his own strengths and weaknesses—in a manner that will equip him for the arduous tasks with which life confronts him" (Henderson 112). According to the structure of the hero archetype, once the protagonist responds to the call to adventure, he is guided and trained for his new life by wise tutelary figures, who are symbolic representatives of the whole psyche. However, in Rusty's story (as was the case with the author), these ministering figures are not the godlike sages or celebrated warriors of epic literature, but teenagers like himself. These powerful friendships do much for his self-esteem and shape his character. By crossing social, cultural, and economic barriers, Rusty acquires humanity and relates to people who are different from himself.

The Room on the Roof also addresses the sensitive topic of the emerging sexuality of teenagers with seriousness and candor, a subject that was neglected during the 1950s in literature about young adults. Rusty falls passionately in love with Mrs. Meena Kapoor, the mother of his young pupil, whom he sees as the mother he has never known. Mrs. Kapoor responds to his adoration at first with motherly affection and then, perhaps because of her frustrated and unhappy life with her alcoholic husband, she is flattered by Rusty's attention and kiss. They are kindred souls: Rusty feels protective toward Mrs. Kapoor because, like her, he was once trapped in a loveless relationship. She is abused emotionally and psychologically by her husband's drunkenness and sense of failure, just as Rusty was abused physically and mentally by Mr. Harrison. Rusty wants to give her the love and attention she deserves, and that he was so sadly denied by his guardian. His awakening love for an older woman is a normal aspect of adolescent sexuality, according to psychoanalysts like Anna Freud. His love "brings with it a resurgence of Oedipal feelings" that prompt him "to idolize his mother [or a mother figure] and to believe that she is more appreciative of him or that she responds to him in a more appropriate manner than his father [Mr. Kapoor, in this case]" (qtd. in Harris and Liebert 484).

The Room on the Roof also succeeds in presenting the adolescent's perspective of adults. Nat Hentoff, in his analysis of books for teenagers, states that "[r]emarkably absent from most fiction for the young is any real density of perception of the ways in which [adolescents] look at and react to the adults with whom they live" (404). Like J. D. Salinger's groundbreaking novel *The Catcher in the Rye* (published in 1951), *The Room on the Roof* portrays the false values, abusiveness, rationalization, and selfishness of adults—both British and Indian—in their dealings with children. With excruciating frankness, Bond exposes the cruelty and hypocrisy of Mr. Harrison and the self-centeredness, indulgence, and neglect of Mr. Kapoor toward his son. Was the teenage author taking revenge on all the adults who had hurt and offended him? Perhaps. Bond admits that Mr. Harrison's character is based on the people he had resented as a teenager: his stepfather, his uncle in Jersey, and Mr. Fisher, the teacher and headmaster at Bishop Cotton School (Interview).

Rusty's secure Indian world is rudely shattered when Mr. and Mrs. Kapoor are in a car accident en route to New Delhi; Mrs. Kapoor is killed, and Mr. Kapoor decides not to return home. Kishen, who was left in Rusty's care, is taken to his aunt's house in Hardwar. Rusty's remaining friends also eventually leave Dehra: Somi goes to Amritsar, and Ranbir and Suri to boarding school in Mussoorie. Although Rusty still has his room on the roof—symbolic of his personal autonomy—the glorious summer of his life is over; he no longer feels part of the busy life in the compound of the house.

Just as Rusty had run away from his British world because it was too confining, he now wants to leave India because he is lonely and depressed and feels he has no roots in the Indian world apart from the immediate physical presence of his friends. He suffers from the postcolonial trauma of displacement when he realizes his tentative position in India—loss of country, sense of exile, yearning for the security of family and friends, and the loneliness of an outsider. Somi tries to convince him to stay in Dehra, arguing that without a birth certificate and passport he has no legal status or nationality: "You are neither Indian subject nor British subject" (114–15). However, Rusty does not believe that an official document can resolve his dilemma: "But I don't belong here, Somi. I don't belong anywhere. Even if I have papers, I don't belong. I'm a half-caste, I know it, and that is as good as not belonging anywhere" (115).

Worried about his future, Rusty embarks on yet another journey of discovery. He reluctantly decides to go to the British High Commission in New Delhi to request an assisted passage to England. On his way to Delhi, he stops at Hardwar to say goodbye to Kishen, only to learn that Kishen has run away from home to become a thief, because he was disillusioned when his father remarried within a month of his mother's death. Rusty's brotherly love for Kishen, and the late Mrs. Kapoor's trust that he would look after her son, prompt Rusty to search for Kishen and assume responsibility for his welfare. Rusty finds Kishen, and the two plan to return to Dehra. Rusty's life now has a sense of purpose: he feels that Kishen and he are "each other's refuge" (144) and recognizes that his roots in India are deep and complex:

> He could not run away. He could not escape the life he had made, the ocean into which he had floundered the night he left his guardian's house. He had to return to the room; *his* room; he had to go back. (145)

Rusty acquires maturity and self-knowledge only after he transcends his personal miseries and problems and makes a commitment to his Indian community, responding with the same loyalty, friendship, and generosity that were earlier extended to him. Before returning to Dehra, Rusty takes a ritual bath in the holy Ganges in Hardwar, a place of pilgrimage for Hindus, symbolizing his baptism into Indian culture and a mystical union with his Indian self.

> Lying on his belly on the river bank, he drank of the holy waters. Then he pulled off his shirt and sandals, and slipped into the water. There were men and women on all sides, praying with their faces to the sun. Great fish swam round them, unafraid and unmolested, safe in the sacred waters of the Ganges. (138)

Rusty now knows that despite his white skin, he belongs to his friends, to India, and to the entire universe. A woman in a ferry boat asks him: "What are you my son, are you one of us? I have never, on this river, seen blue eyes and golden hair." Rusty replies, "I am nothing...I am everything" (114). Although Rusty has found his "home" in the diverse world of India, he has, more importantly, successfully completed his process of individuation, or the "achievement status," according to Marcia. He has resolved his identity crisis; has become a mature and self-confident young man, willing to face the future with hope and courage; and, above all, has developed love and empathy for others. The circular journey motif serves as a metaphor for Rusty's passage from childhood to adulthood, from dependency to responsibility, from self-effacement to involvement with others, from exclusivity to cultural hybridity.

DECONSTRUCTING THE COLONIAL NOVEL

While Bond's personal experiences in Dehra Dun run as a subtext throughout the novel, more significantly *The Room on the Roof* marks the decline of the colonial novel. As Jeffrey Meyers has stated, "the tradition of the colonial novel runs parallel to the rise and fall of Western colonization," and with the end of British rule in India, such a novel "can no longer be a truly vital form" (vii). Written for domestic consumption, colonial literature was propagandist in nature, intended to glorify and rationalize the British Raj in India.[4] Colonial literature dictated that educated and cultured Indians be ignored in the colonial novel, as in social relationships. Instead, Indian characters were stereotyped as childlike, irrational, and lacking in self-discipline; or portrayed as loyal and faithful servants, emphasizing that "natives" are inferior and fit only to serve. Albert Memmi calls this approach a "systematic devaluation of the colonized" (66), and Shamsul Islam sees the master-servant relationship as an "extension of the guardian-child or parent-child relationship" (7). *The Room on the Roof*, in contrast, explores the themes of home, of "isolation from *both* England and India...[and of] being torn between two worlds" (Greenberger 180). The novel subverts the conventions of the colonial novel by satirizing the two British characters in the novel, while presenting a variety of complex and interesting Indian characters. Rusty's friends are genuinely caring, and their interracial friendship is based on equality and mutual respect. Far from depicting Indians as subservient or dependent, Rusty's only hope of survival away from his Anglo-Indian world lies in the help he receives from his Indian friends and their families.

During the Raj, the British had asserted their distinct identity by maintaining their distance from everything Indian. Yet the Anglo-Indian protagonist of *The Room on the Roof* responds to the clash of cultures by moving out of his confined British space to connect with the land of his birth—with the people, places, and culture of India—not in terms of racial superiority but by identifying with the Indian experience; the outsider becomes an insider. Rusty accepts the hybrid nature of his identity, which is due to his "intertwined and overlapping histories," to quote Edward Said (18). In *Culture and Imperialism*, Said further clarifies that "[p]artly because of empire, all cultures are involved in one another; none is single and pure, all are hybrid, heterogeneous, extraordinarily differentiated, and unmonolithic" (xxv).

The Room on the Roof also subverts the derogatory myths of the "primitives." Colonial discourse had proclaimed the superiority of Christianity and did not attempt to study the art, religions, ethical principles, and lifestyles of India. It considered native religions and "pagan" rituals, especially the pantheon of Hindu gods and their worship, barbaric, superstitious, and perverted. An anonymous contributor to the July 1902 issue of the *Quarterly Review* warns readers:

> It is in the religious atmosphere above all of India that the Englishman feels himself to be moving in a mysterious, unrealised world, and this feeling is of the essence of romance. He does well to resist the seduction which this atmosphere exercises upon those too curious about it. (Qtd. in Parry 53)

Yet Rusty is attracted to the "magic" of Hindu rituals: while playing Holi or bathing in the Ganges, he feels a mystical union with everything Indian; he feels at one with creation. Despite the attitude of colonial authors like Kipling, who upheld Western civilization, the post-1935 Anglo-Indian response to India was varied and complex. Once the British Raj had started to crumble, many authors such as Rumer Godden and Iris Macfarlane attempted to subvert imperial attitudes by forging new areas in race relations. For instance, the protagonists of Macfarlane's *The Children of Bird God Hill* celebrate Beehu, the Spring Festival, and perform the symbolically rich *puja* ("prayer ritual") associated with the worship of Lord Krishna, who awakens the world to life with his magical flute. Like Rusty, Macfarlane's characters recognize their links to the past and claim the culture of the land they love. Similarly, M. M. Kaye's autobiography touchingly concludes with her desire to kiss the ground when she returns to India after being in England for nearly eight years (449).

Once Bond received the advance of £50 from André Deutsch, and the assurance of soon seeing his first book in print, he bought a ticket aboard the Polish passenger ship *S. S. Batory* and left for India in March 1955, after spending over three and a half years in Jersey and England. Ruskin Bond's "heroic" journey had come full circle when he returned to India as a published author—and ever since then he has refused to succumb to the temptation of leaving India for more lucrative jobs abroad. He told me that he cannot imagine how people born in India—people whose ancestors have lived and died there—can settle in another country (Interview). In writing *The Room on the Roof,* the young author had vicariously resolved his own cultural ambiguity by defining himself as an Indian of "double" British and Indian heritage: "Being a child of changing times, I had grown up with divided loyalties; but at the end of the journey I had come to realize that I was blessed with a double inheritance" (*Scenes* xvi).

NOTES

1. For an account of his life in Jersey, see Ruskin Bond, "A Year in Jersey," *A Garland of Memories* 28–30; and "Three Jobs in Jersey," *Scenes from a Writer's Life: A Memoir* 139–43.

2. In 1956, Diana Athill also launched V. S. Naipaul, winner of the 2001 Nobel Prize for Literature.

3. This analysis of the novel is a revised version of my article "The Search for an Identity: Journey as Metaphor in *The Room on the Roof,*" which appeared in *The Creative Contours of Ruskin Bond,* ed. Prabhat K. Singh (New Delhi: Pencraft, 1995), 71–81. Reprinted by permission.

4. For more information on the elements of the colonial novel, see Meena Khorana, Introduction, *Africa in Literature for Children and Young Adults: An Annotated Bibliography of English-Language Books.*

WORKS CITED

Athill, Diana. Letter to Meena Khorana, 16 March 2000.
Bond, Ruskin. *A Garland of Memories.* New Delhi: Mukul Prakashan, 1982.
___. Interview with Meena Khorana. Mussoorie, July 1995.
___. *The Lamp Is Lit: Leaves from a Journal.* New Delhi: Penguin, 1998.
___. *The Room on the Roof.* 1956. Rpt. New Delhi: Penguin, 1987.
___. *Scenes from a Writer's Life: A Memoir.* New Delhi: Penguin, 1997.
___. "The Typewriter." Bond, *Lamp Is Lit* 118–21.
___. "What's Your Dream?" Bond, *Garland* 22–24.
Godden, Jon and Rumer. *Two under the Indian Sun.* New York: Knopf, 1966.
Godden, Rumer. *The River.* Boston: Little, 1946.
Greenberger, Allen J. *The British Image of India: A Study in the Literature of Imperialism 1880–1960.* London: Oxford UP, 1969.
Harris, Judith Rich, and Robert M. Liebert. *The Child: Development from Birth to Adolescence.* Englewood Cliffs, NJ: Prentice, 1984.
Harris, Michael T. *Outsiders and Insiders: Perspectives of Third World Culture in British and Post-colonial Fiction.* New York: Lang, 1992.
Henderson, Joseph L. "Ancient Myths and Modern Man." *Man and His Symbols.* Ed. Carl G. Jung. Garden City, NY: Doubleday, 1964. 104–57.

Hentoff, Nat. "Fiction for Teenagers." *Only Connect: Readings on Children's Literature*. Ed. Shiela Egoff, G. T. Stubbs, and L. F. Ashley. Toronto: Oxford UP, 1969. 399–406.

Islam, Shamsul. *Chronicles of the Raj: A Study of Literary Reaction to the Imperial Idea towards the End of the Raj*. Totowa, NJ: Rowman, 1979.

Kaye, M. M. *The Sun in the Morning: My Early Years in India and England*. New York: St. Martin's, 1990.

Khorana, Meena. Introduction. *Africa in Literature for Children and Young Adults: An Annotated Bibliography of English-Language Books*. Westport, CT: Greenwood, 1994. Xiv–xxi.

___."The Search for an Identity: Journey as Metaphor in *The Room on the Roof*." *The Creative Contours of Ruskin Bond: An Anthology of Critical Writings*. Ed. Prabhat K. Singh. New Delhi: Pencraft, 1995. 71–81.

Macfarlane, Iris. *The Children of Bird God Hill*. New York: McGraw, 1967.

Memmi, Albert. *The Colonizer and the Colonized*. Expanded ed. Boston: Beacon, 1991.

Meyers, Jeffrey. *Fiction and the Colonial Experience*. Totowa, NJ: Rowman, 1968, 1973.

Parry, Benita. *Delusions and Discoveries: Studies on India in the British Imagination 1880–1930*. Berkeley and Los Angeles: U of California P, 1972.

Said, Edward. *Culture and Imperialism*. New York: Pantheon, 1978.

Salinger, J. D. *The Catcher in the Rye*. Boston: Little, 1951.

"States of Jersey." Website: <http:// www.gov.je>.

3

Back in Dehra: "The People and Places I Have Known"

Ruskin Bond returned to India as a published author in 1955, with plenty of youthful optimism and self-confidence that he could succeed as a freelance writer in Dehra. When his ship docked in Bombay in March 1955, he took a train to New Delhi, where he was received by his stepfather. He learned that Mr. Hari's business in Dehra had gone bankrupt, hence his mother, sister Ellen, brother William, and two half-brothers were shortly going to accompany Mr. Hari to New Delhi. Because he wanted "a room of his own," Bond decided to remain in the small town in the Doon Valley below the Himalayas, the place he felt was "home" in India, the surroundings of his childhood and young adult memories. In Dehra, he could "be among strangers without feeling like an outsider" (*Scenes* 155). However, the Dehra he loved had changed. Not only had his old friends from 1951 moved out—because "Dehra, then, was not a place for young men in search of a career"—but he regretted that "the march of time and the pressures of population" had destroyed the old lifestyle of Dehra (*Lamp* 12, 55).

Bond rented a room from Bibiji, his stepfather's first wife, an enterprising Punjabi woman who owned a small provisions store on Rajpur Road in the Dilaram Bazaar. Her shop was located in Astley Hall, which had stores on the ground floor and apartments above. Bibiji lived in the back of the store, while Bond rented the room above it, which had a balcony in front that looked onto Rajpur Road. While Bibiji resented her ex-husband and his Anglo-Indian wife, she did not blame

Ruskin and treated him like a member of the family, preparing his breakfast every morning.

Bond would spend much time gazing at the passersby from the balcony, and it became his window to the world. His neighbors in Dehra soon became an integral part of his life and community, and he worked them into his stories. Mrs. Singh, who also lived in Astley Hall, was fond of telling him tales from her village about the supernatural, many of which Bond has retold in his collections *Tales Told at Twilight* and *A Season of Ghosts*. At twilight, Mrs. Singh would sit on her *charpoy* ("string bed"), smoke a hookah, and narrate stories of *churels* ("ghosts of immoral women"); she genuinely believed in ghosts and malignant spirits and had many personal experiences to narrate (see *Lamp* 10–12).

Bond had returned to India with the equivalent of Rs 800. Unlike in London, it would not be easy to get a job in Dehra—or anywhere in India—without a university degree. He realized that if he was to support himself by writing, he would have to produce articles and short stories at a steady rate. Attempting a longer project was out of the question. It had taken him several years to complete his first novel, and although accepted for publication, it did not appear until 1956. Moreover, *The Room on the Roof* did not make him much money at that time (it is more widely read today), even though André Deutsch had sold the serial rights to the *Illustrated Weekly*, where it was serialized in 1956 (with illustrations by Mario). However, Bond had confidence in his ability to write and was determined to succeed at all costs.

In India in the mid–1950s, the only prospect a writer in English had was to publish short pieces in English-language journals and newspapers. The Sunday editions of the leading newspapers published literary supplements that provided an outlet for creative writers in English. However, it was difficult to publish book-length fiction because in the early years of Independence, the few publishers in India focused mainly on educational materials. Even the novels of internationally recognized writers like R. K. Narayan, Raja Rao, Mulk Raj Anand, and Khushwant Singh were mostly published abroad before being reprinted in India. The realities of publishing after decolonization—small readership in English, competition from imported books, domination of multinational publishers, and Indian publishers focusing on "safe" publications like textbooks and supplementary readers—invariably forced an Indian novelist writing in English to win recognition abroad before he or she could hope to be published in India. Furthermore, as Haydn Moore Williams points out, the work of Indian writers has

> a ready-made appeal for readers outside India...[and therefore] most Indians who use English write consciously for readers in England, America, Australia and Canada. Outside India, books about India have a particular exotic appeal....Some Indian writers, fully aware of this appeal, exploit it, piling on local colour, explaining and expatiating upon Indian customs, detailing recipes of Indian dishes, describing sarees and outlining the colourful rituals of an Indian wedding. (xv–xvi)

Under these publishing conditions, Bond figured that if he "bombarded every magazine in the country, [he] could probably eke out a livelihood" (*Scenes* 155). And he proceeded to do just that, sending short stories, essays, and short articles regularly to English newspapers and to the "some half a dozen English language magazines" in India (*Scenes* 155). Bond tried to extend his readership by maintaining his contacts with publishers in London and regularly submitting material to them.

He earned approximately Rs 300–400 a month, just enough to scrape by. He humorously refers to himself as the "champion of Grub Street" (*Lamp* 15) and as Scheherazade because his survival depended on his ability to tell stories (Introduction, *Tales* 9). His essays and articles, which covered a variety of topics such as animals, nature, plants, ghosts, and movies, were published in the literary sections of *The Sunday Statesman* (Calcutta), *The Hindu* (Madras), *The Tribune* (Ambala), *The Pioneer* (Lucknow), and *The Leader* (Allahabad). Some even appeared in nonmainstream publications like *Sainik Samachar* (Armed Forces weekly; New Delhi), which paid him Rs 25 for 1,000 words. For a couple of months, he also contributed a regular column, "Letter from Hollywood," about American movies and new stars, to *The Leader*, for which he was paid Rs 30.

Bond writes that his autobiographical work *The Lamp Is Lit: Leaves from a Journal*, a collection of essays, episodes, and journal entries, is "a celebration of my survival as a freelance—this survival being as much the result of my stubbornness and persistence as of any talent that I may possess" (x). Of those days, he explains:

> At twenty I was a published author, although not many people had heard of me! And although I wasn't making much money then, and probably never would, it was the general consensus among my friends that I was an impractical sort of fellow and that I would be wise to stick to the

> only thing that I could do fairly well—putting pen to paper. (*Lamp* 13)

His early struggles as a freelance writer are fictionalized in the novellas "Delhi Is Not Far" (written in 1960) and "A Handful of Nuts" (written in 1995), which describe the experiences he had during these years. The latter story is more elegantly written. With its tongue-in-cheek style and humorous tone, it assumes an irreverent attitude in portraying the narrator's life and experiences with his "nutty" friends. It also describes the Dehra of the mid–1950s, with the hybrid, postcolonial culture of the middle class and a range of character types from the lower classes.

In spite of Bond's self-deprecating remarks that he was "lazy," he worked furiously during this time. In order to survive as a writer, he had to lead a disciplined life of regular writing; yet he also felt free because he did not have to conform to the set schedule of a job. He would write for a couple of hours each morning, about a thousand words, then he would go to a café for coffee, meet friends, and eat at cheap roadside *dhabas* ("eating houses") near the Clock Tower or at fashionable restaurants. Upon returning to his room in the evening, he would again write a little. His eyesight was weak, yet he had to endure writing by kerosene lamp because Bibiji could not afford to pay her electricity bill. While his life was tough—irregular meals, no family life, and financial insecurity—this lifestyle suited him: he wrote to live, but he also wrote because he loved to do so. "When we are young, we can put up with a great deal of discomfort in order to follow a dream" (Introduction, *Room* ix). Amid all this uncertainty, he felt protected by his father, his guardian angel, a feeling that is presented as a mystical experience in "A Handful of Nuts": "My dear, dear father. How much I had loved him....Now he had given me a sign that he was still with me, would always be with me" (21).

Bond was also in contact with the writers' community in India through the newly founded Writers Workshop in Calcutta. Established in 1958, the aim of the Writers Workshop was to promote indigenous writing in English, to publish creative writing and "transcreations" under the Workshop imprint, and to encourage literary criticism. The Writers Workshop also started a bimonthly journal, *The Miscellany*, that gave preference to unpublished young writers who were talented and innovative. Bond was part of this network of writers who were struggling to project an Indian voice in English. According to Purushottama Lal, secretary of the Writers Workshop, Bond was "one of the three Indian writers in English in India who [made] their living by free-lancing" (211).[1]

THE SHORT STORIES: 1955–59

During this time, Bond established his preferred genre, first out of necessity and practical considerations and then because the short story and novella suited his "style and temperament" as a writer. In the introduction to *Strangers in the Night*, he writes that "the short novel, with its compositional economy and homogeneity of conception, has its place in the scheme of things" (xi). There is restraint and economy in Bond's handling of style; characters are delineated in a few deft strokes, and the plot evolves from a revealing or defining episode. The difference between essays and short stories depends, he writes, "upon whose personality comes through more strongly, the author's or the characters he describes. If it is the author's, then it is really an essay. If it is the characters', then it is a story. Or is that too much of a simplification? In my own case, I have often found my stories becoming essays and vice-versa!" (Introduction, *Delhi Is Not Far* xii).

From 1955 to 1958, most of the short stories Bond wrote were first published in the *Illustrated Weekly*, edited by the Irishman C. R. Mandy, and then submitted to other journals in India, such as *The Sunday Statesman*. Mandy recognized the potential and skill of the budding young writer and encouraged him by publishing most of the stories he wrote during this period (he generally earned about Rs 100 for each story). To get a wider audience, his stories (both reprints and new stories) were also published in a variety of journals abroad, such as *Short Story International* (New York), which specialized in reprints, and *Blackwood's Magazine* (London). His short stories were also broadcast on the BBC in London, in the fifteen-minute short story slot. Several of these stories have become classics and have been anthologized in collections such as *The Night Train at Deoli and Other Stories* and *Time Stops at Shamli and Other Stories*.

Nearly all of Bond's short stories are in the first person, relying heavily on his life for plot, characterization, and themes. His struggles as an author, personalities of his neighbors and friends, and well-known landmarks of Dehra became the subjects of his stories in various forms. "The Window,"[2] first published in *Illustrated Weekly* in 1956, is an excellent example of how he worked his everyday activities and acquaintances into his stories. The window motif, which he had first used in *The Room on the Roof*, symbolizes a vantage point in this story, a feeling of owning the world. The narrator observes the birds in the banyan tree; traffic and people on the path beside the building—vendors, children, postman; and the panoramic view of the city. When a young girl comes to visit one of his neighbors, he befriends her and shares the "magic" of the window with her. "It gave us the power of detachment: we were deeply interested in the life around us, but we were not involved in it" (26). To the protagonist, the window is magical because it offers a mystical vision—almost like the one Lord Krishna gave to Arjuna in the *Bhagavad Gita*. But the young child sees it differently: "it is like a cinema," said Koki, "the window is the screen, the world is the picture" (26). When she has to go back to her hometown, she hopes that he will still be there when she returns, because if he is not, someone else may shut the window—the window to the mind, the window to the heart that lets the world in.

Bond wrote some of his best "train" stories during this period. In "Soot Gets into Your Eyes," the introduction to *The Penguin Book of Indian Railway Stories*, a collection of colonial and post-Independence train stories edited by Bond, he writes that he is not a good traveler by train but that he loves railway platforms because he "spent a great deal of time on them when [he] was a boy, waiting for connecting trains" (xiii). Further inspiration came from his family's close involvement with the Indian Railways—his grandfather, William Dudley Clerke, was assistant stationmaster in Karachi in the 1920s and Fred Clark, his mother's cousin, was the station superintendent at Delhi Main during World War II. A train compartment or a small train station becomes the ideal setting for depicting a transitory relationship and for evoking the Indian scene. In the introduction to *The Night Train at Deoli*, he writes: "I find that in the stories I wrote in the 1950's…there is a good deal of romance, often associated with trains. People are always travelling in them and going all over the place, but just occasionally two people meet, their paths cross, and though they may part again quite soon…their lives have been changed in some indefinable way" (no pag.).

The plots of these train stories focus on the meeting of strangers, the brief acquaintance, the parting, and then the memory. The title story, published in *Illustrated Weekly* around 1957–58, captures the essence of one such fleeting moment with restrained suspense. It is a romantic story about an eighteen-year-old college student who is returning home from college. When his train stops briefly at Deoli, he is attracted to the girl selling baskets on the platform. She has pale skin, shiny black hair, and dark eyes—the symbols of feminine beauty in all of Bond's stories. He gets off, buys a basket, and shyly makes contact with her; and then he gets back on the train as it pulls out of the station. He forgets all about her until the train stops at Deoli on his way to college after the holidays. Both are pleased to see each other, and they look forward to the next meeting. However, when his train stops at Deoli on his way home, she is no longer there. He questions the stationmaster, and then makes a special trip to question the tea-stall owner, but no one knows why the girl has stopped coming to the station. The protagonist feels tenderness and responsibility toward her, and vows to break his journey some day to make inquiries—but he never does. He is afraid to find out what actually happened to her: Did she leave Deoli? Get married? Was she sick? According to Jaishankar Kala, the narrator's "obsession is…sad, innocent, naïve and boyishly saintly" (102). Bond, however, states in the introduction to the collection that "the hero…tries to prevent that moment from passing…but it is only the very strong among us who can alter events, change trains so to speak, and very often cause a derailment" (no pag.). The girl is someone who excites the protagonist's fancy, his sense of mystery, and every time he passes Deoli station, he keeps "hoping and dreaming" (56).

The haunting atmosphere of this story resonates in other important train stories like "The Eyes Have It" and "The Woman on Platform 8," both originally published in *Illustrated Weekly*. "The Eyes Have It" is a cute story about two passengers on a train, one male and the other female; both are blind, yet they carry on a conversation about the weather, not revealing their handicap. It is only when the girl gets off and another passenger enters the compartment that the protagonist learns that she was blind like himself. The story is full of verbal ironies: the protagonist thinks she cannot see that he is blind because he is sitting in a dark corner and because he can call on his memories and other senses to carry on an intelligent conversation; and she does not know that he does not know she is blind. The story also comments on "seeing," because many people who have good eyesight do not have the ability, or the time, to notice details.

"The Woman on Platform 8" is a sensitive portrayal of the loneliness of a young boy on his way to boarding school. Again, the pattern of strangers meeting briefly on a train platform and touching each other's lives forever is repeated in this story. Arun's parents, thinking that he is old enough to look after himself, send him alone to the train station by bus, even though he will have a long wait before he can catch the train at midnight. Their neglect is contrasted with the domineering and possessive manner of a classmate's mother. The ideal mother is the mysterious woman on the platform, a poor but dignified widow who approaches the lonely boy and takes care of his needs without overpowering him with attention or advice. She treats him like a grownup and lets him speak about his likes and dislikes, school, and friends, while the bossy mother keeps warning the boys to beware of strangers—ironically, she does not know that the mysterious woman is a stranger to the boy! When the train is about to leave, Arun leans out and gives the woman a parting kiss and calls her mother, but there is no such display of affection between the classmate and his mother. Who is this mysterious woman and why did she come to the station? There's a hint that her son may have been hit by a train, because she is alarmed when a young boy takes a short cut across the tracks in front of an oncoming engine. Does she come to the station to relive her sorrow or to vicariously experience motherhood by befriending young boys? The story displays Bond's respect for children and his disapproval of adults who patronize them. It also appears to draw on the anguish and inner resentment the author experienced as a boy when his mother did not come to receive him at the train station in Dehra.

Bond also employs the short story to expose social pretensions and the fickleness of people. "The Boy Who Broke the Bank" is a story about small-town gossip and how a serious crisis is precipitated by a chance remark made by a poor boy, who was employed to sweep the bank, that he had not been paid. A middle-class woman interprets the remark to mean the bank has no money. The rumor spreads through the town until everyone begins to withdraw his or her money, and the bank is really on the verge of bankruptcy. It is not just the well-off who are satirized here. Even the lame beggar, Old Ganpathi, who has never been seen to walk, gets up and runs to the bank—he has a savings account! Yet there is no sympathy for Seth, the bank manager, who is heartless, immoral, and exploitative—and he probably gets his just desserts.

From 1956 to the 1960s, Bond also published short fiction for children in *Elizabethan* (London), an excellent magazine for older children. Edited briefly by Kaye Webb (who was also editor at Puffin) and then for a few years by Patricia Campbell, this journal no longer exists. Bond published approximately ten stories in *Elizabethan*, including "The Thief," "The Long Day," and "Stolen Daffodils." Some of these stories were first published for adults in *Illustrated Weekly* before being reprinted in *Elizabethan*. The best known among them is "The Thief," a thought-provoking story about a fifteen-year-old thief, a Robin Hood-type character, who charms his way into working for a writer in return for food and some lessons. When the author gets paid a tidy sum for a story, the boy first steals the money and then has a change of heart. He goes back to return the money because his master is not greedy or rich or poor but a good, trusting person. He is a thief with a conscience, and this hesitation while stealing had got him caught several times. "A successful thief must be pitiless," he says (*Night Train* 42). The writer, for his part, pretends he does not know the money was missing and gives the boy a reward. He also offers to pay the boy a regular salary in the future and to teach him to write sentences, hence giving the vagrant an opportunity to make something of himself. The story raises complex sociological issues about right and wrong, the effect of compassion and forgiveness on people, and the dignity of people considered social outcasts. However, the story is not didactic, because we end up feeling sorry for the thief. He is not punished but rewarded for stealing; the punishment is his inner conflict: "only a terrible sadness not for the loss of money but for my having betrayed his trust" (*Night Train* 41).

It was during this period that Bond wrote an early draft of one of his most popular short stories for adults, "Leopard in the Lounge." Because of its awkward length—longer than a short story and shorter than a novel—it was difficult to get it published at that time. He revised it and published it in 1975 as the novella "Time Stops at Shamli" along with "Love Is a Sad Song" in a slim volume entitled *Love Is a Sad Song*.

VAGRANTS IN THE VALLEY: A FANTASY ABOUT FREEDOM

In 1957 *The Room on the Roof* won the John Llewellyn Rhys Prize, administered by the National Book League (London) and awarded to the "most memorable work of any kind which shall have been published for the first time during the previous calendar year" by a Commonwealth author under thirty (see Singh 208). Bond received £50 as prize money, and rights to the book were sold to the German publishers Albert Langen-Georg Müller (Munich) and to Deutsche Hausbücherei (Hamburg) for a special illustrated edition, for which he was paid approximately £200. This bit of good fortune gave Bond the luxury of beginning a longer fictional piece—and the result was *The Young Vagrants*, the sequel to *The Room on the Roof.* As Virginia Woolf states in *A Room of One's Own*, a writer needs space and financial security to have time to write. *The Young Vagrants*, serialized in *Illustrated Weekly* in 1957 (illustrated by Mario), was not published in book form until 1981. It was reprinted in 1993 as *Vagrants in the Valley*, along with *The Room on the Roof*, by Penguin Books India. It was not a successful novel, but the author states in the introduction that he has "a special affection for it, because it was written at a time when [he] was struggling to make a living as a freelance writer…and consorting with [his] fellow 'vagrants,' some of whom are described in the book" (viii). Both books, Bond continues, are "portraits of adolescence written by an adolescent" (viii). According to him, *Vagrants in the Valley* "lacked some of the youthful optimism of my first book; but it had more of my sensuality" (*Lamp* 6). In a sense, this book is a fantasy about freedom: what would it be like to live entirely on one's own, with no adults, school, or job to dictate to you? Ironically, while Bond was writing this book of two free spirits who are not bound by any conventions or rules, his own life was strictly regulated.

Like *The Room on the Roof*, and unlike the short stories written during this period, *Vagrants in the Valley* is written in the omniscient third person. Its well-integrated plot is also structured in the cyclical pattern of the hero returning home from a journey, hero making a new home, and hero leaving home on another journey. As in the previous novel, the journey motif serves as a metaphor for growth and maturation from adolescence to adulthood. Although there is comfort in the familiar, in order to progress one needs to take the risk of leaving home and facing new challenges. The novel also explores the meaning of home and cross-cultural friendship through Rusty's relationships with his Indian friends.

The story continues where *The Room on the Roof* ends, with Rusty (17) and Kishen (15) returning home to Dehra. Is "home" a sense of belonging to a physical dwelling, such as a room, or is it the comfort of a familiar place, a place where one is loved and where one matters? For Rusty and Kishen, Dehra represents all of these, even though they no longer have any family there. To reach home, they walk, hitch a ride on a bullock cart, ride ticketless on a train, trudge through forest paths, and cross swift mountain streams. When they reach Dehra, their physical homes (Rusty's room on the roof and the house where Kishen had lived with his family) are no longer waiting for them. They have been locked up by the landlord, and because the two boys have no money to pay the rent, they become homeless. Seth, the landlord, is only interested in extracting money; he does not even give Kishen and Rusty a place to stay for the night. They visit Somi's mother (a friend from *The Room*), who gives them a meal and some money, and urges them to stay with her, but Rusty refuses because he wants to be self-supporting. Both sleep in the open maidan that night, and the next day Rusty decides that they will live in the abandoned St. Paul's Church. The two friends now make up a family—Rusty is like a big brother to Kishen—where there is love and caring and commitment for one another. Their family unit is stronger than the ones they had with their biological parent or guardian.

Rusty had run away from an abusive, narrow-minded guardian, and Kishen from a drunken and neglectful father.

The story is a fictionalization of the author's struggles at the time, of his not having a secure home, of being displaced—yet also of being free. Rusty and Kishen live the life of vagrants; they prefer the "risks and pleasures of vagrancy to the security of living with people [they] did not know" (122). Vagrancy, on the one hand, spells romance and freedom on the journey of life, but on the other, it is their only means of survival. M. A. Jeyaraju calls them "hard-headed realists" whose "very vagrancy seems to be, in the ultimate analysis, an inevitable compliance with the reality they cannot escape" (86).

The peeling walls and decaying, overgrown garden of the old church symbolize the shrinking British population and the end of the Raj in India. Rusty "hated to see old things, old people, suffer lonely deaths" (142). To Rusty, the church is a reminder of the social conformity he had disliked as a young child: required attendance at church by his guardian, the boring sermons, and the gossip of middle-aged women. Yet the church is also his past—the people his deceased father and he had known are buried there—and his future. His new life, phoenix-like, will emerge from within the walls of the crumbling church. Rusty's practical consideration is to look for a teaching job in a school in order to support Kishen and himself. And if these efforts fail, he will start writing, because that is the only type of work he wants to do. Rusty's life is also idyllic: he feels one with nature as he bathes in the pond behind the church, and as he lies on a rock to dry off, "the sun was in the pool and the pool was in the sky and the rock had swallowed Rusty up" (213).

Rusty makes friends with other vagrants like himself, and they all come to live in the church. Each has a touching story of how he became homeless. The Sikh boy Devinder's parents were killed during the partition of India in 1947 and, like so many people in Punjab, the political events made him a displaced person. But "Devinder had both his feet planted in the greater world, the open world, the world that is both lonely and free" (163). He sells combs and buttons during the day and studies at night for a university degree. The Goonga ("mute") was abandoned by his family as a child because of his handicap. He lives on the streets at the mercy of people—some hit him and make fun of him, while others feed him. Sudheer, the Lafunga ("loafer"), is a crook who uses his wits to charm money from people, even from the prostitutes Hastini and Mrinalini, and to steal from the rich and greedy. But he is also a victim. As a child, he had wandered into India from the Frontier as a homeless refugee and was adopted by a smuggler, who introduced him to a life of crime. While the author does not overlook Sudheer's immoral and criminal behavior, he is treated with sympathy. These characters portray a very human picture of the sociological and psychological effects of Partition on the lives of displaced children.

Viewed from the perspective of middle-class standards, these characters are delinquents or, at best, irresponsible. Bond criticizes social pretensions and narrow-mindedness by giving a sympathetic portrait of the underdogs of society, by seeing beauty in what society rejects. These vagrants befriend each other for their humanity and do not look through the mirror of social success. There is genuine friendship, loyalty, and a strong sense of family among them. Racial and cultural differences are of no consequence to them—the state of vagrancy acts as the social equalizer. Although life is culturally different in the Indian world (clothing, food, bathing habits), Rusty adapts easily and is comfortable in it. Their experiences provide a glimpse into an uninhibited and carefree life, but they also have to be alert, to use their intelligence, knowing whom to trust. The vagrants are in no "hurry to get anywhere. They had everywhere to go, and they could take their own time going there, and there was no one to hurry them on" (163). Rusty's philosophy is that to live a life of vagrancy, one needs to have time, but then one cannot have money.

However, not all adults are uncaring. Somi's mother had offered her home to Rusty and Kishen; even the self-righteous and domineering Mrs. Bhushan is willing to look after Kishen because she had been a friend of his mother. Because the future is uncertain and because Rusty realizes that Kishen needs a secure life, he convinces him to stay with Mrs. Bhushan's family and continue his studies. Life in her home is comfortable—all Kishen's physical needs are taken care of—but it is also a jail compared to the freedom of vagrancy. This brief stint as a vagrant has made Kishen less selfish and has given him a glimpse of the open world and the needs of others.

Just as Kishen has found a benefactor in Mrs. Bhushan, Rusty meets Mr. Pettigrew, a pukka British sahib, who loved hunting tigers in his youth and whose house is full of the memorabilia of his past. Though not a vagrant or homeless, Pettigrew is also a displaced person. Like many older Anglo-Indians, he stayed on after Independence because he loved India and because he could not start life anew in England. Pettigrew, who knew Rusty's father well, serves as a father figure to Rusty, offering him advice and money, and telling him about an aunt who may have a valuable memento from his father.

Within the novel's circular structure, there are two shorter journeys that Rusty takes from Dehra. Each trip teaches him something about his past or helps him to make a decision—such as not to take the easy path of staying in the safety of home or of becoming dependent on others. Accompanied by Sudheer, he goes to the Garhwal hills to look for his Indian aunt, the widow of his father's younger brother. He finds her living alone with only a servant to care for her needs. Like Pettigrew, she appears to be lonely and living in the past; she sits alone on her verandah smoking a hookah, just as Pettigrew sits in his cane chair with his pipe and whiskey. She tries to convince Rusty to live in her home, so that they can look after each other, but Rusty wants to be independent. Both Pettigrew and Rusty's aunt are individualists, but the price they pay for their independence is loneliness. Rusty wonders: "Weren't there any permanent flesh and blood companions to be found outside the conventions of marriage and business?" (215). He does not want such a fate for himself, but he accepts that freedom and loneliness are part of this "open world." His aunt gives him the books his father had left for him. One, *Alice in Wonderland*, which had belonged to his grandfather, turns out to be a rare first edition, which Pettigrew thinks might sell for over £600.

From his aunt's house, Rusty goes to the pilgrimage town of Rishikesh with Sudheer. While Sudheer thinks it is a good town in which to hide from the authorities and to con rich people by posing as a *sadhu* ("ascetic"), Rusty resolves to leave the life of vagrancy. "I want to give some direction to my life. I want to work, I want to be free, I want to be able to write. I can't wander about the hills and plains with you for ever" (210). Rusty is confident that he has made the right decision because he feels one with the Himalayan mountains; he "loved these hills, which offered him their freedom, their own individual strength, allowing the boy to be himself, Rusty" (201).

The novel ends on a realistic note when Rusty returns to Dehra and the "family" of vagrants breaks up and they all go their separate ways. Vagrancy is a temporary phase, one that has to end when adult responsibilities or the necessity of earning money are faced. While homelessness spells freedom from conventions, Rusty had always known that "he would soon tire of this aimless wandering" (198) and that "[y]ou can't be a vagrant for ever....He had to stop now, and find a place for himself, or go forward to disaster" (214). He is aware of the importance of money for survival and for personal dignity, but he is not obsessed with it.

He fails to get a job in Dehra, and there is no chance of finding one anywhere in India because he does not have a university degree. It is an age of specialization, and the only skill he has is with words. As Pettigrew suggests, his only option is to go to England; the money from the sale of his rare book will give him the freedom to find his true profession. The novel ends with seventeen-year-old Rusty embarking on yet another journey to find his identity and to fulfill his dream of becoming a writer—and he can always return home if things don't work out. The farewell at the train station in Dehra connects all the characters and episodes of the plot. After seeing him off, his friends were "pleased that Rusty's life had taken a new direction; they were impressed by his good fortune, and they took it for granted that he would come back some day, with money and honours. Such is the optimism of youth" (222–23).

Vagrants in the Valley evokes a sense of place through telling descriptions. From the bazaar scenes of Dehra, to the solitary villages in the Himalayas, to the saffron-robed sadhus at their morning ablutions and meditations in Rishikesh, and to the crowded train compartment, the novel recalls the sights, smells, and "soul" of this region. The description of the Ganges in Rishikesh is especially evocative: "The broad, slow-moving Ganges caught the moonlight and held it, to become a river of liquid silver. Along the shore, devotees floated little lights downstream" (203). The atmosphere of the village in the Himalayas is equally poetic: "he saw mountains, blue and white-capped, with dark clouds drifting down the valleys. Pale blue woodsmoke climbed the hill from the houses below, and people drifted about in the warm winter sunshine" (183). The novel also captures the essence of the simple rustic folk and the urban characters: the beauty and charm of the village girl whose "bangles made music when she moved her hands—it was as though her hands spoke a language of their own" (201); the bus driver who carries on a heated political discussion instead of watching the road; the rum-drinking villager who cures sheepskins; the wrestlers practicing in the public pit, who are "on their knees, arms interlocked, pressing forward like mad bulls, each striving to throw the other" (205); and the dancing girl-prostitute, who says: "The more people I see, the lonelier I get" (207).

This novel is intricately linked to *The Room on the Roof* not just through the setting and references to events and characters from the earlier novel, but also through the extra background information provided on Rusty's childhood and family. These details lend texture and depth to the story and connect them to the author's life: Rusty learns from Pettigrew that his father loved the world of nature, collected rare books, and was a romantic and sensitive man—an actual portrait of Bond's father. Pettigrew also talks about Rusty's childhood and how he preferred reading the books he found in a forest resthouse to going on hunting trips with his guardian—again, reminiscent of a similar trip the author had taken as a young boy. Likewise, Rusty's aunt recounts his family history and details of his own babyhood. When she gives him the books his father left for him, he remembers his grandfather's bookshelf and his father reading to him under the shade of a jackfruit tree.

With *Vagrants in the Valley* and the shorter pieces written in Dehra, Ruskin Bond had carved a niche for himself as a writer. In the introduction to *The Night Train at Deoli and Other Stories*, he outlined his aesthetic credo, saying that he preferred to write about "the people and places I have known and the lives of those whose paths I have crossed. This crossing of paths makes for stories rather than novels, and although I have worked in both mediums, I am happier being a short-story writer than a novelist" (no pag.).

NOTES

1. Ruskin Bond has published two verse collections with the Writers Workshop: *It Isn't Time That's Passing* (1972) and *Lone Fox Dancing* (1975).

2. All quotations from the short stories discussed in this section have been taken from the collection *The Night Train at Deoli and Other Stories*.

WORKS CITED

Bond, Ruskin. "Delhi Is Not Far." Bond, *Delhi* 353–428.

___. *Delhi Is Not Far: The Best of Ruskin Bond.* New Delhi: Penguin, 1994.

___. "A Handful of Nuts." Bond, *Strangers* 1–80.

___. Introduction. Bond, *Delhi* vii–ix.

___. Introduction. Bond, *Room* xi–xiv.

___. Introduction. *Tales and Legends from India.* 1982. New Delhi: Rupa, 1990. 9–11.

___. *The Lamp Is Lit: Leaves from a Journal.* New Delhi: Penguin, 1998.

___. *Love Is a Sad Song*. New Delhi: Orient Paperbacks, 1975.

___. *The Night Train at Deoli and Other Stories*. New Delhi: Penguin, 1988.

___. *"The Room on the Roof" and "Vagrants in the Valley": Two Novels of Adolescence.* New Delhi: Penguin, 1993.

___. *Scenes from a Writer's Life: A Memoir.* New Delhi: Penguin, 1997.

___. *A Season of Ghosts.* New Delhi: Viking, 1999.

___. "Soot Gets into Your Eyes." *The Penguin Book of Indian Railway Stories.* Ed. Bond. New Delhi: Penguin, 1994. Xi–xvi.

___. *Strangers in the Night: Two Novellas*. New Delhi: Penguin, 1996.
___. *Tales Told at Twilight*. Bombay: India Book House, 1970.
___. *Time Stops at Shamli and Other Stories*. New Delhi: Penguin, 1989.
___. *The Young Vagrants*. Bombay: India Book House, 1981.
Jeyaraju, M. A. "Home sans Roof: Celebration of Vagrancy in *Vagrants in the Valley*." Singh 82–86.
Kala, Jaishankar. "The Saint and the Garbage Can." Singh 100–02.
Lal, Purushottama. "A Dedicated Young Talent." 1966. Rpt. Singh 211.
Singh, Prabhat K., ed. *The Creative Contours of Ruskin Bond: An Anthology of Critical Writings*. New Delhi: Pencraft, 1995.
Williams, Haydn Moore. *Studies in Modern Indian Fiction in English*. Vol. 1. Calcutta: Writers Workshop, 1973.
Woolf, Virginia. *A Room of One's Own*. 1929. New York and London: Harcourt, 1957.

4

The Transitional Years: 1959–63

Ruskin Bond's five years in Dehra were very difficult because of financial hardship. He recalls in his autobiographical collection *The Lamp Is Lit: Leaves from a Journal* that Dehra "was going through a slump; it would recover only a decade or so later" (5). In 1959 he decided to leave Dehra and move to New Delhi to look for a regular office job, as he had done in Jersey and London. In Delhi[1] he lived mostly with his mother and stepfather, first in the Rajouri Gardens locality and then in South and East Patel Nagar, where they later moved. He did not have a job the first year he was in Delhi, but for the next three years he worked for Cooperative for American Relief Everywhere (CARE), the international relief agency. This was an office job that also involved a lot of traveling to refugee centers—such as to Mysore in the south and to the Tibetan resettlement camps in the north—an experience that heightened Bond's empathy for the suffering of displaced people. (He met the Dalai Lama briefly on one of his trips.) His responsibilities included writing project reports, which were later sent to CARE headquarters to be evaluated for funding.

During his five years in Delhi, from 1959 to 1963, he published a few short stories for children but mainly essays and travel pieces for adults. The demands of a daily job left him very little time for a long creative project or to prepare all his manuscripts for publication. However, he never gave up the discipline his father had instilled in him of recording his experiences, thoughts, and impressions in his journal, a habit he still maintains. Some of these entries would later serve as source material for his novellas, short stories, and essays.

Although this was a transitional period—and quiet as far as any major publication is concerned—it was an embryonic time when he was traveling extensively in India, absorbing the subtle nuances of Indian lifestyle, researching his Indian and British heritages, and formulating concepts. It was also a period of self-definition and the identification of "home" in India—was home in Dehra in the Doon Valley or in the metropolis of Delhi, with its jobs and opportunities and attendant complexities? Bond missed the comparative peace and quiet of Dehra and found Delhi to be crowded, dusty, and hot. Post-Independence Delhi had changed tremendously since the time when he had lived there with his father as a child. The capital was also reeling under the massive influx of the enterprising Punjabi refugees from Pakistan. The resulting crowding, noise, and speeding traffic did not appeal to him, and he took every opportunity to take nature walks, visit old tombs and historical monuments, and to explore the uninhabited parts of Delhi and its surrounding villages.

His stay in Delhi provided valuable insights into the burgeoning Punjabi middle class and the aggressive atmosphere of post-Independence Delhi—the rush for material prosperity and success at the personal level and industrialization and progress at the national level. His essay "Walking the Streets of Delhi," based on these experiences and later trips to Delhi, captures the atmosphere of urban Delhi with its frantic activity. For instance, the pavement of one commercial street is described as being crowded with vendors, lottery stalls, giant cinema billboards, and small eating places; with a variety of people plying their trade (gypsy blacksmiths, people making straw mats for roofs, a Pathan selling aphrodisiac); and with a dead pony, hit by a truck, being pecked by crows. Always in tune with his personal response, Bond sensitively reveals the dignity of people who have to live in squalor and regrets that materialism and the desire to get rich have made people apathetic toward human suffering.

Bond formed a strong emotional attachment to his mother and stepfather's Punjabi neighbors in Rajouri Gardens, the Kishore family. The essay "Bhabhiji's House," originally published in the early 1970s in *Blackwood's Magazine* and later reprinted in *The Lamp Is Lit*, is a lively account of a day in the life of the Kishores (called Kamal in the essay). With subtle irony, the essay points out the underlying tensions as Bhabhiji, as head of this extended family, controls the at times contradictory desires and needs of the various members of her large middle-class household of three sons, two daughters-in-law, fourteen grandchildren, a married daughter whose husband is in England, and visiting relatives. Yet there is love, commitment, and unity among them—and Bhabhiji is that bond. Bond visited the family often, even after leaving Delhi, because of his friendship with a grandson of the family, Anil Chopra (son of Bhabhiji's daughter), whom he guided through life and who is now a physician in the United States. Also, Bond fell in love with Bhabhiji's granddaughter, Shashi Kishore, to whom he would later propose marriage. This proved to be a defining experience in his life and gave him much cause for frustration with the system of arranging marriages, an experience he was to later fictionalize in the novella "Love Is a Sad Song."

In 1960 Bond wrote the short story "The Crooked Tree" and the novella "Delhi Is Not Far," which fictionalize his struggles as a freelance writer in Dehra and rationalize his reasons for moving to Delhi. The novella was not published until 1994, when it was included in the collection by the same title, *Delhi Is Not Far: The Best of Ruskin Bond.* In the introduction, he states that the novella was rejected in India because publishing longer fiction was still not economically viable, and in England and the United States due to its short length and perhaps because of the bisexual nature of the protagonist (xiii). There are no graphic sexual scenes, or even an emphasis on sex in the novella, and Bond later abbreviated it into the short story "Bus Stop, Pipalnagar," which was first published in *The New Renaissance* (Arlington, MA) and later included in the adult anthology *Editor's Choice: Literature and Graphics from the US Small Press, 1965–1977.* This version eliminates the episodes related to the prostitute and the homosexual relationship of the protagonist, but it includes a satirical account of a small-town political rally.

"Delhi Is Not Far" is a fictionalization of the difficulties Bond faced while trying to make a living as a writer in Dehra. Like Bond, the protagonist faces the dilemma of integrity versus personal gain and refuses to compromise his principles for the sake of making money. The episodic plot focuses on the protagonist's relationship with his friends and neighbors in a lower-class locality of Pipalnagar, and his struggle to survive as a writer of murder mysteries. Individual chapters work in short contemplative paragraphs on the uplifting influence of mountains, musings on friendship and death, and vignettes providing information on Lord Krishna, lepers and beggars, and prominent landmarks of Delhi. While the novella seems choppy and hurriedly written at times, this diverse material is unified through the protagonist's dream of going to Delhi to procure a job and of writing a "real" novel. His friends also share his dream of succeeding materially in Delhi. Finally, the protagonist is offered a job by an editor and he moves to Delhi. "The moment the bus was out of Pipalnagar, and the fields opened out on all sides, I knew I was free; that I had always been free; held back only by my own weakness, lacking the impulse and the imagination to break away from an existence that had become habitual for years" (417). He realizes that he has been stagnating in Pipalnagar and that he needs to venture forth, to take risks in order to achieve his dreams.

The significance of this work lies in its slice-of-life portrayal of a poor neighborhood in small-town India: "In Pipalnagar there is not exactly despair, but resignation, an indifference to both living and dying" (363). There is implied social commentary in the protagonist's utter lack of caste and class consciousness in his choice of friends, who form an integral part of his daily life: Suraj, the student and seller of knick-knacks; Deep Chand, the barber; Pitamber, the cycle-rickshaw driver; Aziz, the owner of a small junk shop; and Kamla, the prostitute. Although poor, they are generous and hospitable toward one another and share whatever they have with their friends. The characters are delineated with sensitivity and compassion. For example, Suraj, a victim of Partition, is haunted by his childhood memory of being separated from his parents after they had escaped the communal violence in Pakistan. His frail and sickly body (he is epileptic) is symbolic of the sadness and death he has witnessed, yet his pursuit of education symbolizes hope for the future. Even prostitutes, pickpockets, thieves, and beggars—the dregs of society—are presented as likable and sympathetic characters. Without being too harsh or judgmental, Bond exposes the hypocrisy and pretensions of socially acceptable characters—the landlord who has a mistress and operates a brothel; or middle-class families who make the protagonist feel rejected, like a "piece of driftwood" (375), because he is a bachelor and does not have relatives. The novel's contemplative style will prompt readers to look within and think about their commitment to friends and the meaning of life. The protagonist's sexual relations with Kamla and Suraj become a metaphor for "seeking through sex something beyond sex—a union with all mankind" (406). He sees his friendship with Suraj as a meeting of minds and souls: "In moments of rare intimacy two people are of one mind and one body, speaking only in thoughts, brilliantly aware of each other" (413).

Many distinguishing traits of Bond's fiction become apparent in this novella. He is loyal to his characters (just as he is loyal to his friends and neighbors), hence the same characters or character-types (sometimes with different names) appear in several stories, essays, and novellas for both adults and children. Two of the characters that first appeared in *Vagrants in the Valley*—Goonga and Devinder (renamed

Suraj)—feature in this story as well. This intertextuality produces the effect of meeting old friends in new contexts, and each time we learn just a little bit more about them. "Delhi Is Not Far" has clearly emerged from Bond's sense of dislocation and displacement in a big city like Delhi. He develops this small town–big city dichotomy into a literary trope that will recur in various forms throughout his future works. The big city represents Bond's dissatisfaction with the fast-paced life that he believes is not in tune with the environment. While the small town may have its darker side—corruption and exploitation by people in power—it is nevertheless a symbol of a simple lifestyle and harmony with nature. This manichean tension between the big city and small town or village also evokes a romantic yearning for the past.

EXPLORING A DUAL HERITAGE

Once Bond felt a little more settled in Delhi, he started exploring the nearby towns and researching their history and other distinctive features. This journey explored two distinct paths: his Indian heritage and the past history of the British and Europeans in India. Accounts of his trips to Agra, Rishikesh, Aligarh, Mathura, and Jaipur were recorded in his journal in the early 1960s and later collected in *The Lamp Is Lit*. "The byways of history have always fascinated me," he writes. "The history books tell us about Delhi, Calcutta, Madras and Bombay, but they have little to say about the drama that takes place in the lives of those living in villages or small towns. There are stories to be told about all these places" (*Lamp* 55).

Each essay provides not only a description of the place and its historical or legendary background but also the highlights of Bond's personal visit and the lived experience of the people in modern times. "Rishikesh" is a typical example of this approach. In describing this temple town on the banks of the holy Ganges, he gives details of the drive up to Rishikesh by bus, the variety of pilgrims and *ashrams* ("free temple accommodation for pilgrims"), the hundreds of sadhus in their saffron robes, rituals along the banks of the river, descriptions of the town, and his treks into the surrounding villages and mountain passes. Into this very readable account, he weaves descriptions of nature, anecdotes from mythology and history associated with the region, and information on the local economy. Bond takes an irreverent and ironic stance in trying to determine human motivations. He asks: What brings the ascetic to Rishikesh? Is it because of tragedy, stress, failure, or profit? He would later explore this question in depth in the novella "The Sensualist: A Cautionary Tale."

Visiting Rishikesh and other pilgrimage sites gave Bond an intimate knowledge of Hindu mythology, its gods and their ritual worship, and Hindu beliefs and practices. In "Mathura," he presents the atmosphere of another holy city, this time on the banks of the Yamuna River, where Lord Krishna was born; in "Jaipur," he describes the unique design and architecture of Jaipur, one of the oldest planned cities in the world, and analyzes the impact of history on the town's commercial activity and the character of the people today; and in "Break of the Monsoons," he captures the united response of all creation to the first monsoon rain after the heat and dust of the long summer.

Bond's trips to towns like Shahjahanpur, Meerut, Bharatpur, and Sardhana enabled him to explore his Anglo-Indian heritage. Whenever he could spare time from his office job, he researched the activities and lives of Europeans in India before the establishment of the British colonial government. The result was a series of nonfiction articles that were published in English-language magazines and newspapers in India. In 1969, twenty of these articles were published as the collection *Strange Men, Strange Places*, and in 1992 they were republished after further enhancement. In the preface, the author states that these biographical accounts, all derived from historical sources, are about "those odd, colourful (and admittedly not very 'great') soldiers of fortune—mostly European—who strutted across the Indian subcontinent during the eighteenth and nineteenth centuries" and fought not for "their country, or the East India Company, or even their paymasters—at least, not for long" but for "their own hand, for their own enrichment, for their own greater glory—and sometimes, simply because they liked fighting" (xi). It is delightful to read the articles as a group, because then one can piece together the history of trade and colonization in India, beginning with the exploits of these swashbuckling, romantic adventurers who rendered service to Indian princes or to the East India Company, whichever proved more advantageous to them, and ending with an account of Simla and the romance of trains during Kipling's time (1870s and 1880s).[2]

Interestingly, the subjects of these biographies are mainly "unusual" historical personages, especially Europeans who had in some way bridged the East-West cultural divide or had made firm efforts to do so.[3] The underlying theme of *Strange Men, Strange Places* is that while these heroes may be little known in history books, they played a pivotal role during the tumultuous times when the Mughal Empire was weakening and the independent kingdoms of the Marathas, Rajputs, Jats, Rohillas, Sikhs, and others were struggling to gain power in the vacuum. Further upheavals were caused by the Company's interference in local politics and its territorial expansion with the help of its large army. Many Indian rulers (there were approximately 500 independent princely states in India) engaged European mercenaries in their armies or commissioned them to raise a battalion or corps either to help them gain greater power or to oppose British expansion. In "A Great Soldier: Benoit de Boigne," Bond asserts that had de Boigne (1751–1830), a French soldier of fortune in the employ of Madhavrao Sindhia, not returned to Europe and had Sindhia not died, the British may not have been able to establish themselves in India.

From these accounts, readers can formulate an integrated narrative of the social, economic, military, and political activities of the Europeans in India. Conflicts often arose when these European mercenaries joined the Company's army, because of differences in national and religious affiliations. For example, the essay "Pistols at Twenty Paces: A Duel at Poona" recounts the harassment the Catholic Irishman J. S. Sarsfield had to endure when he joined a Protestant Irish regiment. In order to put an end to his ordeal, he challenged the paymaster to a duel, and he died without firing a shot. Since dueling was illegal, it was customary to report such sudden deaths as being caused by an attack of cholera. Several of these characters appear in each others' stories, since their paths often crossed either because they served on the same side or because they were fighting the enemies of their employers. One of the most colorful characters was Claude Martine (1732–1800), the French "shrewd opportunist" who made a profitable career in the courts of Oudh and through investments in the Company's industries. To repent for his self-interest and questionable means of accumulating his fabulous wealth, Martine instructed in his will that his palace in Lucknow be converted into a school (called La Martiniere, where Bond's mother studied for a short time) and that two additional schools be established in Calcutta and in his native Lyons, charitable works that have made his name immortal, at least in India. Other articles provide interesting information on the adventure and danger in the lives of mail runners under the Mughals and the Company, the history of the Company's wine, the origin of punch in India, and how the drink became popular with the Company men.

As the Company's influence expanded, Christian churches and religious services also began to be established, although churchgoing was not a priority. From "The Story of 'Bombay Church'" we learn that in St. Thomas's Cathedral in Bombay (building started in 1672 by Sir Gerald

Aungier, president of the East India Company's factories, and completed in 1718) the sermons were often used for political libel rather than for moral edification. This essay and "The Story of a Hill Station," which traces the development of Mussoorie from a convalescent site for soldiers to a fashionable Himalayan summer resort, provide a context for understanding Victorian author Mary Martha Sherwood's dismay at the moral and spiritual neglect of the British soldiers and children when she came to India with her husband's regiment in 1805. According to Janis Dawson, a Sherwood scholar, "Missionary work had not been encouraged by the company, and as army officers were not known for their religious enthusiasm, there was little interest in schools, teachers, or religious services" (273). The daughter of a clergyman and a tireless volunteer in the Sunday School Movement, Mrs. Sherwood immediately organized classes in religious instruction and started writing her missionary novels set in India, among them the well-known *Little Henry and His Bearer* (1814).

The biographies also emphasize the cultural hybridity of these characters and their acceptance of Indian culture. In "Glories of the Hookah," Bond points out that "[t]his was a period when Englishmen readily took to Indian customs and pastimes, a happy attitude that was to disappear with the advent, in the following century, of Victorian prudery and Christian evangelism" (77). They adapted to Indian customs *and* maintained their European ways: many studied Persian and Urdu; smoking the hookah was fashionable among men and women in Bengal; and there were no social taboos against marrying a Hindu or Muslim woman, because there were few European women in India during these early days. "Colonel Gardner and the Princess of Cambay" narrates the intrigues and adventures of Colonel William Linnaeus Gardner, who served in the armies of the Marathas and married a Muslim princess; "The Lady of Sardhana" describes the exploits of Begum Samru, who married Walter Reinhardt and had affairs with other Europeans after his death, led troops into battle, and converted to Catholicism; and "Skinner and His Yellow Boys" focuses on the "restless and high-spirited" Eurasian James Skinner (1778–1841), who combined his English habits with a harem of Muslim wives, literary creations in Persian, and building a church, mosque, and temple.

These short biographies are based on the diaries, histories, and other rare and out-of-print books that Bond found in secondhand book shops or in private collections in India. He also traveled to most of the cities where the action took place and visited the churches, cantonments, and Christian cemeteries to corroborate what he had read, and often to find new information. "History is best enjoyed...by visiting the scene of actual events, and allowing one's imagination to roam backwards and forwards in time" (Preface, *Strange Men* xi). Bond's summation of Colonel Gardner's career in "Colonel Gardner and the Princess of Cambay" can apply to all these individualists: he was "equally at ease in both worlds," because "Englishmen had not yet developed the social and moral priggishness which was to become characteristic of the Victorian era" (6). With the establishment of the colonial government, Bond emphasizes that the British attitude toward India changed to one of exclusivity and the "White man's burden."

THE EUROPEAN DIASPORA: *A FLIGHT OF PIGEONS*

Bond's continued investigation into his British heritage would eventually culminate in the historical novel, *A Flight of Pigeons*, which he drafted while still in Delhi. It was published in the November 1975 issue of *Imprint*, the magazine he was editing at that time. The story focuses on the stormy events that swept through northern and central India during the 1857 rebellion against the British. This nationalist movement began in Meerut on May 10, 1857, when the Indian soldiers in the Company's forces rose against their officers and took charge. Soon the resistance spread to other cantonment towns and throughout the princely states, challenging the Company's annexation of or interference in their kingdoms. The novel provides both the British and Indian interpretations to these events: the first-person account sensitively presents the impact of the violence on innocent Europeans, while the political and social uprisings indicate that it was not an isolated "mutiny" of the *sepoys* ("soldiers") but a grassroots freedom movement that was orchestrated by leaders of all segments of the population, both Hindu and Muslim, army and civilian.

The small town of Shahjahanpur, about 250 miles from Delhi (where Bond's father was born), serves as a microcosm of the events that occurred throughout north-central India in 1857. Bond's trips to Shahjahanpur enabled him to re-create the setting where the events took place, giving details of the parade ground, church, and cantonment as they must have been nearly 150 years ago. Although well-researched, the novel does not overpower readers with facts. The center of interest is focused on the fate of two Eurasian women who are caught in the holocaust: Ruth and her mother Mariam, who is of mixed French and Muslim blood and the wife of the Frenchman Mr. Labadoor. The unfolding events are based on the actual experiences of a Ruth Labadoor, a fourteen-year-old girl of mixed Indian and French blood, whose diary was privately published as *Mariam* by J. F. Fanthome, to whom she had related her experiences. Bond read Fanthome's book on the Mutiny, where portions of the diary are quoted, the *Shahjahanpur Gazetteer* of that year, and other accounts of the Mutiny that made references to Ruth Labadoor. While staying faithful to the facts, Bond gives his interpretation of this momentous historical event by juxtaposing the experiences of the protagonists in the European, Hindu, and Muslim worlds. With his typically ironic vision, Bond reveals how the mixed racial heritage of the Labadoor women affects their sociopolitical status. They are accepted as members of the European community of Shahjahanpur, yet once the freedom fighters reach Shahjahanpur on May 31, that very fact endangers their lives. Now it is their Indian background that will save their lives and prompt them to seek shelter in the humble homes of the Hindus they know.

Mariam, who has always treated her Indian servants and vendors with respect and kindness, and who is kept abreast of the local gossip and vital information about the Indian resistance, has already made arrangements in case they have to flee. The Europeans are attacked while the church service is in progress at St. Mary's. Mr. Labadoor is killed, along with many British officials and their families, but Ruth escapes and joins her mother in their hiding place. In order to survive, the women shed their European identities and put on Indian clothes, and Ruth takes a Muslim name, Khurshid ("sun"). After hiding in their Hindu benefactor's house for a month, Ruth, Mariam, and other members of their extended family are caught by Javed Khan, one of the Muslim leaders of the resistance in Shahjahanpur; however, he cannot bring himself to kill Ruth. He takes them to his home because he admires Mariam for protecting her daughter and because he has been infatuated with Ruth's beauty for many months.

> Like an enraged tigress, whose side has been pierced by a barbed arrow, she hurled herself at me and presented her breast to my sword. I shall never forget the look she gave me as she thrust me away from the girl! I was awed. I was subdued. I was unmanned. (850)[4]

As guests of Javed Khan's Muslim household, Ruth and Mariam assume Muslim identities, and they gradually become less European. Mariam's impressive Muslim ancestry, her knowledge of Muslim culture, and their ability to speak fluent Urdu enable them to communicate with and be trusted by Javed Khan's family.

While the events are given from the perspective of Ruth, the heroine is undeniably her mother. Mariam is kind, clever, resourceful, and dependable. She uses her wits to protect her daughter from the amorous intentions of Javed Khan, reputed to be a cruel yet romantic individual of some wealth and position. He now proposes marriage to Ruth and wants to make her part of his *zenana* ("harem"); yet his sense of honor and good nature will not allow him to take Ruth by force. Mariam uses subtle diplomacy to pacify the jealousy of Javed Khan's wife, ensure their personal safety, and prevent Ruth's marriage to their host and protector. The story dispels mutual stereotypes that Muslims and Europeans have of each other. The Muslim women "were agreeably surprised to find that we delighted in hard work, that we loved needles and thread, and that, far from seeking the company of men, we did our best to avoid them" (865). Readers, too, will get an intimate picture of Muslim culture: interaction between males and females, rituals of bathing and washing hair, courteous language, protocol of receiving and returning visits of relatives, the ritual of singing songs and playing on swings after the first rains, and storytelling. This depiction of a Muslim household is very different from the uncharitable, stereotypical portrayal in colonial novels like *Tiger Burning Bright*, by Theodora DuBois.

The situation is once again fraught with irony when the British forces quench the rebellion and capture Delhi, the seat of the Mughal Empire, and imprison the ailing emperor, Bahadur Shah Zafar. It is now the Hindu and Muslim nationalists and their families who must flee Shahjahanpur. When the victorious British army takes control and the Indians are running away, Ruth and Mariam, who are still under Javed Khan's protection, cast off their Indian clothes and are happy to assume their European identities and privileges. Suspense and tension are effectively employed in narrating the story of their escape until they are safe in Mariam's brother's house in Bharatpur. Throughout their ordeal, Ruth and Mariam are helped by the British, Hindus, Muslims, and Sikhs. These are life-changing experiences for the protagonists, and they come to realize the futility of war—both sides burn and loot houses, riot and rape, and kill innocent women and children. Mariam promises to use her influence to protect Javed Khan's family and to prevent British retribution against him.

While the ending is "happy" for the two main characters, the novel is not necessarily optimistic about the future. A bond has been forged with their protectors that makes Ruth and Mariam understand Indian resentment against foreign rule and that its continuation would lead to much unhappiness. We know from history that the British Crown took control of India only a year after the rebellion erupted, and that British reprisals were just as cruel and ruthless. The title of the novel also has a double meaning: the imagery of a flock of white pigeons who hover over the city, circle in the air when disturbed, and come down to rest again is a metaphor for the British presence in India and this temporary disturbance. However, when Javed Khan accidentally shoots a white pigeon perched on a tomb, it signals an ill-omen for him—and for the nationalist forces.

A Flight of Pigeons bridges barriers by giving a human face to historical events. Atrocities are committed by both sides in an impersonal manner, yet when the enemies are encountered as real people, they are seen as innocent victims of circumstances and given protection. Ironically, all the Europeans who survive in the story do so with the aid of their Indian servants. The Redmans hide in the house of their washerwoman, and two Muslims risk their lives to bury the dead Europeans in the church. In fact, Mariam's half-brother, Pilloo, prefers to continue living with his Hindu protector and is adopted by him. As Kamini Dinesh writes, "the final impression is that of the essential humanity of man—one that knows no barriers of caste, creed or race" (94).

NOTES

1. The term Delhi is generally used by Indians to refer to both the old city of Delhi (seat of the Mughal Empire) and New Delhi (the new capital built by the British in 1911). Delhi is known as the "Phoenix City," because it was the capital of nine different empires, beginning with the time of the *Mahabharat*, when it was called Indraprastha. The name "Delhi" originated in AD 400 when King Dilleep conquered Indraprastha and renamed it Dilli Pur. For further information, young readers can refer to Emily Polk's *Delhi: Old and New*.

2. The article "Kipling's Simla," which was written later in Mussoorie, was included in the 1992 edition of *Strange Men, Strange Places* because of its thematic relevance to this collection.

3. Also refer to Kate Teltscher, *India Inscribed: European and British Writing on India 1600–1800*.

4. All quotations from *A Flight of Pigeons* are from *Collected Fiction*, by Ruskin Bond.

WORKS CITED

Bond, Ruskin. "Bhabhiji's House." Bond, *Lamp Is Lit* 31–44.

___. "Break of the Monsoons." Bond, *Lamp Is Lit* 45–48.

___. "Bus Stop, Pipalnagar." *Editor's Choice: Literature and Graphics from the US Small Press, 1965–1977.* Ed. Morty Sklar. Iowa City: Spirit That Moves Us, 1980. 203–25.

___. "Colonel Gardner and the Princess of Cambay." Bond, *Strange Men* 3–8.

___. "The Crooked Tree." *Ruskin Bond's Treasury of Stories for Children.* New Delhi: Viking, 2000. 281–93.

___. "Delhi Is Not Far." *Delhi Is Not Far: The Best of Ruskin Bond.* New Delhi: Penguin, 1994. 353–428.

___. *A Flight of Pigeons.* 1980. Rpt. in *Collected Fiction.* By Bond. New Delhi: Penguin, 1999. 823–98.

___. "Glories of the Hookah." Bond, *Strange Men* 77–80.

___. "A Great Soldier: Benoit de Boigne." Bond, *Strange Men* 33–43.

___. "Jaipur." Bond, *Lamp Is Lit* 72–75.

___. "Kipling's Simla." Bond, *Strange Men* 85–90.

___. "The Lady of Sardhana." Bond, *Strange Men* 9–15.

___. *The Lamp Is Lit: Leaves from a Journal.* New Delhi: Penguin, 1998.

___. "Love Is a Sad Song." *The Night Train at Deoli and Other Stories.* By Bond. New Delhi: Penguin, 1988. 210–37.

___. "Mathura." Bond, *Lamp Is Lit* 65–71.

___. "Pistols at Twenty Paces: A Duel at Poona." Bond, *Strange Men* 1–2.

___. "Rishikesh." Bond, *Lamp Is Lit* 57–64.

___. "The Sensualist: A Cautionary Tale." *Strangers in the Night: Two Novellas.* By Bond. New Delhi: Penguin, 1996. 81–143.

___. "Skinner and His Yellow Boys." Bond, *Strange Men* 22–29.

___. "The Story of a Hill Station." Bond, *Strange Men* 56–60.

___. "The Story of 'Bombay Church.'" Bond, *Strange Men* 30–32.

___. *Strange Men, Strange Places.* 1969. New Delhi: Rupa, 1992.

___. "Walking the Streets of Delhi." Bond, *Lamp Is Lit* 21–30.

Dawson, Janis. "Mary Martha Sherwood." *British Children's Writers 1800–1880.* Ed. Meena Khorana. Detroit: Gale, 1996. 267–81.

Dinesh, Kamini. "*A Flight of Pigeons*: The Waifs of History." *Creative Contours of Ruskin Bond: An Anthology of Critical Writings.* Ed. Prabhat K. Singh. New Delhi: Pencraft, 1995. 87–95.

DuBois, Theodora. *Tiger Burning Bright.* New York: Farrar, 1964.

Polk, Emily. *Delhi: Old and New.* Chicago: Rand McNally, 1963.

Sherwood, Mary Martha. *"Little Henry and His Bearer" and "The Last Days of Boosy."* 1814 and 1842, respectively. Rpt. Worthington, Engl.: Henry E. Walter, 1962.

Teltscher, Kate. *India Inscribed: European and British Writing on India 1600–1800.* 1995. Rpt. New Delhi: Oxford India Paperbacks, 1997.

5

"The Great Escape to the Mountains"

In 1963 Bond gave up his job in Delhi and went to live in Mussoorie, a small town located in the foothills of the Himalayas, where he still resides. He was tired of working at an office job, and he decided that if he was going to fulfill his dream of becoming a full-time writer, he would have to do so while he was still young and able to take risks (Introduction, *Our Trees* x). He chose Mussoorie because it was a relatively inexpensive hill station in those days, before it became a "rich men's playground" ("Writer" 2). He was "not attracted to Mussoorie as a town, but to the surrounding hills, forests, and streams, or maybe to the people from the villages" (Interview). He lived in Oakland Cottage for one year, then rented the second floor of Maplewood Lodge, attracted by its location away from the town on the edge of an oak and maple forest and by the sounds of birds and other animals. Miss Ripley-Bean, an 86-year-old British woman living on a meager pension, occupied the first floor. Situated at about 6,000 feet above sea level, Maplewood Lodge gave him the feeling of being alone with nature, and he especially liked its windows opening onto the forest. In the introduction to *Our Trees Still Grow in Dehra*, he writes that it was a "timeless sort of a place" and that he felt an immediate emotional connection to the natural scenery around the cottage.

> ...and when I pushed the first [window] open, the forest seemed to rush upon me. The maples, oaks, rhododendrons,

> and an old walnut, moved closer, out of curiosity perhaps. A branch tapped against the window-panes, while from below, from the ravine, the deep-throated song of the whistling thrush burst upon me. (x)

"The old cottage was kind to a struggling young writer," he continues about Maplewood, and that is where he wrote most of the stories collected in *Our Trees Still Grow in Dehra, The Night Train at Deoli and Other Stories*, and *Time Stops at Shamli and Other Stories* (xi). Some of these stories had first appeared in *Short Story International, Blackwood's Magazine, The Illustrated Weekly of India, The Sunday Standard, Asia Magazine*, and various other newspapers and magazines in India and abroad.

Another turning point came when Prem Singh became a part of his life. In "From Small Beginnings," included in *Our Trees Still Grow in Dehra*, which is dedicated to Prem Singh and his family, Bond narrates how Prem Singh, at age sixteen, asked for help in finding a job. Since Bond was employing Prem Singh's uncle at the time, he got Prem Singh a job elsewhere, but after a few years Prem Singh took his uncle's place and began working for Bond. Prem Singh came from a village near Rudraprayag in Pauri Garhwal on the higher peaks of the Himalayas. In this rugged area each family owns a small plot of land on which to grow its own food, but money is needed for consumer items. Men join the Army or look for jobs in the towns and cities in the plains below, while women cultivate their small farms and raise the children. Prem Singh married when he was eighteen, so that his mother would have another pair of hands to help with chores. However, when he came to work for Bond in 1971, his wife, Chandra, and infant son Rakesh also moved to Maplewood Lodge because, as Bond says, "Rakesh stole my heart, and I did not let them go back" (Interview). Prem Singh and Chandra took over full charge of running Bond's home and caring for his needs, giving him time to devote to writing. Bond writes that Prem Singh "brought much love and laughter into my life, and what more could a lonely man ask for?" Because he was accustomed to living as a bachelor, he says "[i]t wasn't service that I needed but companionship. In the cottage it was very quiet. The ghosts of long dead residents were sympathetic but unobtrusive" ("From Small" 89, 91).

Bond lived in Maplewood Lodge until 1975 or 1976, when the trees were "slaughtered" and the mountain blasted to build a road. Also, the house was now associated with sadness because Prem Singh's second son, Suresh, had died there of tetanus when he was two. Bond and his adopted family moved further up the mountains to Landour, located at 7,500 feet above sea level; however, it was a little too far from the schools. In 1981 he rented the top floor of Ivy Cottage (which he would eventually purchase in 2002), about 500 feet lower down, where he still lives.[1] He says Ivy Cottage is "a crumbly old building, threatening to fall at any time," but it is conveniently located near the schools and the bazaar (Interview). Also, it is high enough in the mountains for a lonely walk in the hills, so that he can continue to live amidst trees and birds and insects. The house seems to have blended in with the environment; it "lean[s] towards the mountain as if to hug it" (R. Khorana 57) and "provides a dual vision of the highest Himalayan peaks towering above like gods and of the plains visible in the distance below" (M. Khorana 254). Today, Bond lives a conventional family life with Prem Singh, Chandra, their three children, two daughters-in-law, and three grandchildren. The children call him *dada* ("grandfather"), giving him "a feeling of belonging to a family, something which [he] hadn't known since childhood" ("Writer" 3). He writes that although he "live[s] in simple, even austere conditions" (*Rain* 250), he is content to be in the midst of this happy family and seldom wants to leave home. He still sees himself as the goalkeeper from his soccer-playing days at Bishop Cotton School—"providing, protecting, defending home territory, rather than being an aggressive goal-scorer or go-getter" (*Rain* 246).[2] Prem Singh has recently built a house on the outskirts of Mussoorie to accommodate his growing family. "I should probably end up living there too," says Bond, "although I will retain Ivy Cottage as a writer's studio" (Interview).

Bond's first ten years in Mussoorie were difficult. Not only was he once again struggling to survive as a writer, but he also suffered personal loss when his mother died of breast cancer in 1969; his half-brother Harold died in a car accident in December 1970; and his second half-brother Hansal died in a motorcycle accident in 1971. His brother, William, left India around 1965 for the United Kingdom (where he took the accountancy examination), and later settled in Canada. His sister, Ellen, continued to live with his stepfather and stepsister, Premela, and since Mr. Hari's death in the early 1980s, she has been looked after by Premela. (The RAF still sends an allowance for her.) His journal entries hint at the financial difficulties he experienced during this time, yet he was not willing to compromise his freedom as a writer: "I doubt if I have ever written a story or essay or workaday article unless I have really wanted to write it. And in this way I have probably suffered materially, because I have never attempted a blockbuster of a novel, or a biography of a celebrity, or a soap opera that goes on forever" (*Lamp* 195). Several times he was in despair that he would have to take on a job again, but then Hamish Hamilton (London) bought the rights to an unpublished story, "Sita and the River," giving him the freedom to pursue his goals as a writer.[3]

Ruskin Bond has been living in Mussoorie for nearly forty years now, and he has made the Himalayas a part of his life and work as a writer. He has found his "place of peace and power" on a grassy, pine-topped slope facing Pari Tibba (Hill of Fairies); it is the place where he meditates, is inspired to write, and where he communes with the trees: "It's a big world and momentous events are taking place all the time. But this is where I have seen it happen" ("From Small" 83, 84). Amidst such surroundings, he is free to live a simple yet spiritually rich life because, as he says, "[w]hen you have received love from people, and the freedom that only the mountains can give, then you have come very near the borders of heaven" ("Writer" 4). He participates fully in the simple life of the region, frequently taking the pilgrim trails to nearby towns and villages and sleeping at roadside tea shops or at a village school.

Bond is by inclination a nature poet, but since writing poetry is not lucrative, he continues to be a prolific writer of short stories, essays, travel pieces, and novellas—and he finds endless material in the people, places, animals, and plants of the Himalayas. Bond has also become a historian of the region, researching little-known facts about the past of Mussoorie and its surroundings and recording legends and anecdotes told to him by the hill folk and the old British residents.

THE HIMALAYAS: "A LADDER TO HEAVEN"

Living in Mussoorie gave Bond yet another opportunity to explore his dual British and Indian heritage. One of the first hill stations to be settled by the British, Mussoorie provides important links to understanding British expansion and colonization of India and the lifestyle of its early Anglo-Indian residents. Bond has written the definitive history of this hill station in *Mussoorie and Landour: Days of Wine and Roses*, a handsomely produced book that recounts the past (and present) of the twin hill stations of Mussoorie and Landour. According to the author, it is a nostalgic book that "attempt[s] to preserve that which was good in the past" because "[t]he past has served us well: let us serve it in this way" (front matter). Bond is not glorifying or justifying colonial rule in India; rather, he reconstructs the history of this mountain resort because the past is still alive in the old buildings, landmarks, and legends.

The book consists of nine chapters and is liberally illustrated with visually pleasing color and black-and-white photographs by Ganesh Saili, a professor of English literature and a good friend of Bond's. The first chapter, entitled "Birth of a Hill Station," traces the 225-year-old history of the region, from 1765, when Gurkha warriors from Nepal first entered the Kumaon and Garhwal region, to 1815, when the entire Doon Valley was annexed by the British. The remainder of the book is a detailed account of how Mussoorie "came into existence in the 1820s...when the families of British colonials began making for the hills in order to escape the scorching heat of the plains" (9); and how the settlers tried to re-create what they missed of "home" in their mansions, lifestyle, and social activities. Bond presents valuable factual information on all aspects of the emerging town, but he makes it come alive by narrating the exploits of the colorful individuals who lived in Mussoorie and Landour. The chapter on British cemeteries poignantly captures the lives of Anglo-Indians, stating that "the lonely graves with their touching epitaphs of forgotten men and women have a very human story to tell" (27). Another chapter, "Looking for John Lang," provides an interesting account of John Lang, the first Australian-born novelist, who spent the last years of his life in Mussoorie, and of Bond's extensive search to locate his grave at the Camel's Back Cemetery in Mussoorie. Like Kipling, Bond portrays the social life and activities of the Anglo-Indian community with humor and underplayed satire. Unlike Simla, which attracted the "official" crowd, Mussoorie in 1884 was considered a "bold, bad place" (58)—where people came mainly for pleasure or business—and its summer season was enlivened by intrigues, gossip, love affairs, scandals, and an occasional murder. When comparing this account of Anglo-Indians to Bond's earlier essays collected in *Strange Men, Strange Places*, one notes a significant shift in the British attitude toward India, from interaction between the races to one of exclusivity. Also reproduced in *Mussoorie and Landour* is Lang's article "The Himalaya Club," which appeared in the March 21, 1857, edition of Charles Dickens's *Household Words*, and extracts from the booklet *A Mussoorie Miscellany*, written and published by H. C. Williams in the 1930s. Both articles present a satirical "insider's" view of the Anglo-Indian community. "We are all idlers at Mussoorie," writes Lang. "We are all sick, or supposed to be so; or we have leave on private affairs" (266).

There is evidence of painstaking and thorough research in *Mussoorie and Landour*. Bond has read several original sources, including the journal of Emily Eden, sister of Lord George Eden, who was Earl of

Auckland and Governor General of India from 1835 to 1842 (MacMillan 75). However, the book is not a dry recounting of historical details. Bond enlivens his research with anecdotal accounts of the past and present residents of the town, the changes that have taken place since Independence, and the symbols of the Raj that have remained in the old buildings (now converted into hotels and schools), British lifestyle, and British-style public schools for which Mussoorie is renowned even today. In typical Bondian style, the author connects his personal encounters with these landmarks and his pleasure in walking amid nature (as opposed to "the ugly bazaar" and "concrete jungle" [9] that Mussoorie has become today) to the experiences of his friends and neighbors, making the book an invaluable record of the history of Mussoorie and Landour as rendered in human terms.

The Indian side of Mussoorie's heritage is recorded in *Ganga Descends*, a collection of sixteen essays based on Bond's research and travels in the Garhwal hills. The book celebrates the majesty of the Himalayas (Sanskrit for "abode of snow"), the world's greatest mountain mass, which extend some 1,500 miles from east to west; describes the economy and lifestyle of the remote villages; and narrates his excursions to historical landmarks and famous Hindu pilgrimage sites. Bond's many trips to the higher elevations of the Himalayas introduced him to the stories of the hero-gods of the Sanskrit epics and to Hindu mythology, because the Himalayas are revered as sacred dwellings of the gods, and the Hindu shrines in this region are associated with their deeds. The places described in *Ganga Descends* are not on the regular tourist map; only a lover of nature or an ardent pilgrim would brave a trip there. Each essay describes the natural scene and local people with loving care and the lucidity of a poet. Of Bond's prose style, Rukun Advani writes, the "sentences are moist with dew and the mountain air, with charm, nostalgia and underplayed humour" (qtd. on back cover).

It was after coming to Mussoorie that Bond became a lover of nature, and his writings reflect the deep kinship and serenity that he experiences in the midst of the mountains. While he rejoices in the natural beauty of their individual manifestations—the source of the Ganges River as it "bursts from its icy womb" ("Ganga Descends" 64), sounds of birds and mountain rivers, the towering deodar trees, and flower-strewn valleys—his love for the Himalayas is rooted in their permanence, their ability to "keep their secrecy and reserve, remaining remote, mysterious and spirit-haunted" ("Village" 13). The mountains were no doubt instrumental in shaping Bond's pantheistic outlook toward life. There he becomes aware of the oneness of creation: "Rivers, rocks, trees, plants, animals and birds, all play their part, both in mythology and in everyday worship. This harmony is most evident in these remote places, where God and mountains co-exist" ("Magic" 48). Bond has repeatedly stated that he has become a part of these mountains. In "Great Trees of Garhwal" he states: "Quite frankly, I would just as soon worship the deodar as worship anything, for in its beauty and majesty it represents Nature in its most noble aspect" (71). Bond's sentiments are in harmony with Hindu beliefs, because the Himalayas are also considered "a deity in the Hindu pantheon," according to Priyadarsi Dutta. The Hindu "view towards the Himalayas," she continues, "is a corollary to seeing god in every atom of the universe" (12).

Bond's love for the unspoiled Himalayan region and the simple life of the rural folk who live there should not be confused with the Western concept of "primitivism." While he believes that the people of this region are in tune with the rhythms of nature, he does not subscribe to the evolutionist jungle paradigm that the hill folk are "our untamed selves, our id forces—libidinous, irrational, violent, dangerous" (Torgovnick 8). Nor does he conform to Allen J. Greenberger's theory that in the post–1935 period, "[o]nly in the jungles can these last British writers find an India in which they still feel they have a place. Settings such as this will either have no Indian population or be populated by very primitive people" (188). Bond's many trips to this remote environment should not be viewed as the stereotype of the colonial's archetypal journey into humankind's primeval past, an earlier stage from which the Anglo-Saxons had evolved. He is not a deracinated White man trying to reconnect with his instinctual human spirit; rather, he is a worshipper of nature who admires the "innocence of mountains, high places which have retained their power over the minds of men because they still remain aloof from the human presence, barely touched by human greed" ("Sensualist" 134).

Bond complains that "the Himalayas do not appear to have given rise to any memorable Indian literature, at least not in modern times" ("Writer" 2).[4] Not surprisingly, he is the only contemporary author who consistently turns to the Himalayas as a source of inspiration for his stories. The villages and manifestations of nature described in *Ganga Descends* form the settings of many of his stories for children and adults. For instance, the village of Manjari, described in the essay "A Village in Garhwal," is the setting for *Panther's Moon*; and the valleys and mountains around the temple of Tungnath are the background against which the elemental struggle for survival in *The Eyes of the Eagle* takes place. The natural surroundings shape the personalities and lifestyle of his characters, who "have long since learned humility and patience," and yet "these are cheerful sturdy people, with great powers of endurance. Somehow they manage to wrest a precarious living from the unhelpful, calcinated soil" ("Village" 13, 14). Bond's simple literary style, sensitivity that imbues even the most insignificant object or event with great importance, gentle, humanistic attitude, and spiritual approach to living are shaped by his long association with the mountains.

STUDIES OF SMALL-TOWN INDIA

Bond's early short stories written in Mussoorie were mainly character studies of the distinctive individuals he had come across in the small towns and villages of northern India. Except for the years spent in London and New Delhi, Bond has always lived in small towns in India, hence these vignettes emerge from his keen observation of and emotional engagement with Indian society. The collections *The Night Train at Deoli and Other Stories*, *Time Stops at Shamli and Other Stories*, *Our Trees Still Grow in Dehra*, and *Friends in Small Places: Ruskin Bond's Unforgettable People* contain several portraits of the Anglo-Indians he has known, his neighbors from Astley Hall in Dehra, and a variety of small-town professionals like kitemakers, police inspectors, wrestlers, and tonga drivers. In the introduction to *Friends in Small Places*, Bond states that he finds these people interesting "[n]ot because they were of great importance or stature but because their individuality made them stand out from the commonplace. It was not money or success but pride in themselves that set them apart" (vii). While he presents a diverse range of character types, they can be categorized according to those who represent a bygone era, those who are considered failures by society's standards but who live by their own rules, and psychological portraits that reveal what influences the behavior and motivations of people.

The first type of character provides glimpses of good people of the past and, in some cases, how the sweeping changes taking place in modern society have made them irrelevant. "The Prospect of Flowers"[5] describes the sad plight of elderly Anglo-Indians who stayed on in India after decolonization. Written in the early 1970s at Maplewood Lodge, which inspired the setting, it is the story of Miss Mackenzie, who lives on a small pension in a remote cottage surrounded by her garden. "She knew she would not fit in with the life of post-war Britain. Her home was in these hills, among the oaks and maples and deodars. It was lonely, but at her age it would be lonely anywhere" (114). While her fading life symbolizes the end of an era, she still has something valuable to offer to an Indian schoolboy who trespasses in her garden. Anil represents youth, energy, and curiosity—qualities that Miss Mackenzie no longer possesses—but she has knowledge and experience of the rare Himalayan plants that he is passionate about. Their friendship is a touching reminder not only of the interdependence of the old and the young but also of how an era that has passed can enrich and inform the one that follows.

"The Garlands on His Brow" focuses on Hassan, a small-town wrestler who is admired for his skill. At the prime of his career, he succumbs to the sexual advances of a Rani and gives up his profession for a life of ease in the palace. When the Rani dies, he returns to the *akhara* ("public wrestling pit"), but in the years he was away, wrestling has changed from an art to a competitive sport, and he is no match for the professionals. In order to survive, he first tries teaching wrestling to children and then is reduced to beggary. The prominent themes that surface in the story are exploitation of simple small-town characters and the failure of society to care for its past heroes; they are ignored, forgotten, and allowed to die, because "life had since become fast and cruel and unreflective, and people were too busy counting their gains to bother about the idols of their youth" (82).

Likewise, "The Kitemaker" also evokes nostalgia for the past because craftsmen like Mehmood, who once designed rare kites that resembled dragons or that made music, are no longer patronized. No one has the leisure, inclination, or open spaces for such sports in this "swiftly changing and competitive world" (103). However, Mehmood, like Miss Mackenzie, has passed on his love for the dying art of kiteflying to his grandson, Ali. As is typical of Bond, the descriptions of the likable characters employ images, comparisons, and metaphors taken from the world of nature. Hence, the kitemaker is likened to the banyan tree, "his hands gnarled and twisted like the roots of the ancient tree" (104). Since these characters represent a bygone age, they die at the end of the story. Miss Mackenzie falls sick and dies on a cold winter night, her spirit flying to the mountains that she had always wanted to climb; Hassan commits suicide by crawling into a drain, head first, and no one except the protagonist recognizes him; and Mehmood dies while dreaming of a majestic kite he would make for his grandson.

Bond has also portrayed some very independent characters in defining moments of their lives, when they disregard society's standards of success and uphold a higher law. Their actions challenge readers' engagement at the moral level, whether to suspend judgment against the protagonists or to condemn them outright. In "A Case for Inspector Lal," Keemat Lal, a small-town police inspector who is a failure in his profession, describes his most interesting case to the narrator, who is an author. Bond deftly employs form and voice to distance himself from the speaker *and* ensure the imaginative sympathy of readers to the inspector's point of view. The confessional-type format immediately draws readers into the inspector's account of the investigation of the Rani's murder and his reasons for not arresting thirteen-year-old Kusum, the tailor's daughter, who confesses to killing the Rani out of self-defense when she was being forced into prostitution. The inspector prefers to let the case remain "unsolved." We are repulsed by the behavior of the Rani who traffics in young girls and agree with the inspector that Kusum had killed in innocence. There are two laws operating in the story: the law of the legal system and correctional institutions, which Keemat Lal believes would destroy Kusum's spirit, and the higher moral law. However, the inspector does get his comeuppance from society for placing his personal convictions above his duty to uphold societal laws—he loses a promotion and is posted to a small town he dislikes.[6]

Another short story in which the central character takes justice into his own hands is "A Job Well Done," the story of Dukhi, the old gardener. Set during the British Raj, the events are narrated by an eight-year-old Anglo-Indian boy. The stepson of Dukhi's employer, Major Summerskill, the boy looks up to Dukhi. The conflict in the story arises when Major Summerskill orders Dukhi to cover up the well in the garden, and Dukhi is reluctant to do so. To Dukhi, the well represents the past, the necessity of water during summer, a haven for a colony of pigeons, and memories of his late master who loved to sit by the well and make nature drawings. Major Summerskill, who has married the widow of his former master, is an unimaginative individual who rejects anything creative as weak. When the Major returns from a military field trip, he is angry because the job is unfinished and threatens Dukhi with "retirement." Dukhi asks him to look in the well, and when he does so, gently pushes him in and covers the well. The child narrator, who hates his stepfather, is a tacit partner in this crime because he witnesses everything from his hiding place in the tree but tells no one. Dukhi is not punished, and the disappearance of the Major is attributed to other reasons. The loss of the Major proves to be good, because his widow's new suitor is a man Dukhi and the boy approve of. The first-person narrative enables the author to conceal his views on the crime, but his implied sympathy for Dukhi and the boy is apparent. Dukhi, who is a good judge of character, is protecting the memsahib and the boy out of loyalty to his late master. In addition, as someone who works with the soil, he has the wisdom to acknowledge the supremacy of nature. One recalls his statement that the well was there before the house was built, and the Major's complaint to Dukhi that the garden is "[m]ore jungle than garden" (126). The moral ambiguity of the ending has disturbed some readers who believe that Dukhi should have been arrested for murder. The story could also be read in Freudian terms as an expression of the author's repressed hatred toward his own stepfather and his resentment toward his mother for leaving his father and marrying someone who was so different. In analyzing the situation as an adult, Bond believes that his stepfather "was a man without any imagination, and it just did not occur to him that a child might need more than food and clothing. My mother's sensuality was, I think, stronger than her intelligence" (*Rain* 245).

Among Bond's most intricate and thought-provoking stories are the ones that focus on the psychological impact of childhood experiences on the behavior and attitudes of his characters. In the introduction to *When Darkness Falls and Other Stories*, he states, "If our genes have shaped our biological make-up, our environment has shaped the development of our natures" (vii). "Most Beautiful" explores the complex inner life and struggles of a mentally handicapped child who has to put up with the cruelty of the boys in the bazaar and the indifference of his father. "Death of a Familiar" is the story of an intelligent and charming youth, Sunil, who becomes an irresponsible, exploitative, violent, immoral, and sexually promiscuous troublemaker. In spite of Sunil's faults, Bond paints a sympathetic portrait of him because Sunil is the product of the disruption caused by Partition, Anglo-Indian public schools, seeing too many movies, and parental inadequacy. Sunil is ready to change when he falls in love with Maureen, an Anglo-Indian schoolteacher in her thirties; however, his character is not strong enough to follow through, and she marries someone more "suitable." From then on, Sunil's life takes a downward spiral and he ends up being murdered for seducing the wives of two of his friends. This tragic end leaves the narrator wondering whether Sunil had "unsuspected depths of feeling and passion" (100), and whether he had contributed in some way to his friend's downfall.

These studies of small-town characters reflect Bond's nostalgia for the past, for the charm and innocence of an old-world atmosphere. They also uphold traditional values, a simple lifestyle, and respect for the dignity of humble folk. The trope of simplicity and stability of small towns versus the flux and complexity of city life adds depth and meaning to the individual stories as well as projecting the author's worldview. "Small towns don't change in the way that cities change. It is still possible to find the old landmarks and sometimes the old people," the author declares in his introduction to *Time Stops at Shamli and Other Stories*. "They are the heart of India," yet they are "largely ignored except when elections come round" (9). What would happen if a town remained absolutely the same without any interaction with the outside world? Would that be the ideal place? Just such a possibility is explored in "Time Stops at Shamli," Bond's highly acclaimed novella about small-town India.

The story does not focus on one character but on an entire community that is caught in a time warp. Shamli can be reached only by road or train, but the train stops there only briefly (no one gets on or off the train) "before rushing on into the forests" (35). The narrator, a poor Anglo-Indian writer, decides to investigate what happens in Shamli "behind the station walls" (36). Given Bond's literary usage of the city–small town dichotomy, one would expect Shamli to be a peaceful and serene place, away from the frantic activity of large cities; however, its atmosphere is almost eerie. There is none of the hustle and bustle of a typical Indian station, and it seems equally deserted outside the station, except for a solitary tonga and its driver. The old decaying hotel, where the narrator spends one day, is the microcosm of the town. He meets an odd assortment of people who room there, people who are lonely and suspended in their pasts: the alcoholic Miss Deeds, who came to marry a captain but was rejected; Mr. Lin, who is frustrated because the World War prevented his becoming a concert pianist; Satish Dayal, the ineffectual and unimaginative hotel manager; Daya Ram, the all-purpose servant who cannot leave because he has not been paid in three months; and the old gardener, Heera, who had been in Shamli before it became a town. The most intriguing character is ten-year-old Kiran, the daughter of the factory manager, who has something "old and wise" about her.

To make his presence in Shamli credible, the narrator invents the story that he is trying to trace an Anglo-Indian friend, Major Roberts, who is a "romantic, a man with a dream...who gave a damn for money and politics and cities, and civilizations, who was his own master, who lived at one with nature knowing no fear" (59). And now a mind game begins. Mr. Lin claims to know Major Roberts, and he proceeds to concoct a friendship with this imaginary person. The protagonist thinks that a "happy man wouldn't take the trouble of inventing friendships with people who didn't exist, he'd be too busy with friends who did" (45). Ironically, he does not realize that the remark applies to him as well, because Major Roberts is what he wants to be. When he meets Mrs. Dayal, and she turns out to be his old love, Sushila, who is married to the much older hotel manager, we realize that the narrator also has unfulfilled dreams. The two reminisce about their past, and the old passion revives. He offers Sushila a chance to escape from Shamli with him, but she says that her marriage, although unhappy, is tolerable and she does not want to upset social conventions. He is not particularly disappointed when she does not show up at the train station the next morning: "Unattainable, Sushila would always be more bewitching and beautiful than if she were mine" (66). The only one who wants to break away from Shamli is Kiran; she has the ironic vision and distance necessary not to be engulfed by the decaying atmosphere of the town. The narrator's trip to Shamli proves to be an experience of self-discovery, and he gladly boards the train because otherwise he may be caught in the time capsule of Shamli.

The timelessness of Shamli is presented ironically. On the one hand, Shamli is described at the beginning as "a small station at the foot of the Siwalik hills, and the Siwaliks lie at the foot of the Himalayas, which in turn lie at the feet of God" (35). On the other hand, the narrator witnesses the unchanging monotony of the residents' lives, the town's bankrupt economy, and the pervading sense of sadness and decay. Heera's explanation is that Shamli could not thrive as a town because "the jungle was bigger than the town" (48). In the short time that the narrator spends in Shamli, a leopard takes off with Heera's dog and a part of the hotel roof and wall collapse in a terrible thunderstorm, almost as though the jungle—or nature—is encroaching on the town and trying to reclaim it. The author's statement in the introduction to *Time Stops at Shamli and Other Stories*—"For it isn't time that's passing by, my friend; it is you and I" (10)—gives a hint that timelessness does not mean that "time stops," as it does in Shamli, but that timelessness is part of the eternal scheme of things, where physical time is irrelevant. The timelessness of Shamli could have been experienced *before* it became a town, when it was still in harmony with the jungle. The jungle, the hills—all will endure; it is the people and the towns they establish that are transitory, that appear briefly on this "scene" and then pass.

STORIES OF LOVE AND ROMANCE

In Bond's love stories, the paths of two individuals cross briefly on life's journey; they are attracted to each other but there is no fulfillment or lasting relationship because, just as quickly, their paths fork away. It is a story of unrequited love where the "joy" of the lover lies in remembering past happy moments rather than in possessing the object of his love. As Bond writes in the introduction to *The Night Train at Deoli*, it is about "that longing for something, someone, just out of reach" (no pag.). The male protagonist treasures the memory of the brief encounter as a perfect love that could have been. Bond's brief affair in London with Vu-Phuong, who suddenly left town and never came back, is the prototype for all his love stories (refer to Chapter 2).

Using this basic structure, Bond presents a whole range of love stories from the carefree and natural love between a male and a female, to a love hampered by the restrictions placed on the female by her family, to one in which the female's spontaneous feelings are corrupted by social considerations. The love stories, always told in the first person, mostly involve an unnamed protagonist in his thirties who falls in love with a young teenager. While a relationship between two individuals with such a vast age difference may disturb some readers, suggesting sexual abuse, this is far from the case. It is a mutual relationship where the youth of the female partner denotes an age of innocence, a state of pure, unrestrained love when she gives in naturally to her physical and emotional needs. For instance, Ulla in "The Girl from Copenhagen" is as free as nature in expressing her emotions, and the atmosphere she exudes is "fresh and clean, like the earth after spring rain" (501). She is not seductive when she takes off her clothes and gets into the narrator's bed; and there is an unrestrained, primeval quality to their lovemaking that represents the beginning of time, "like two children who have been playing in the open all day" (501). Their relationship is "transient but complete within itself," writes Aijaz Haider (128). Likewise, the simple girl from the hills in "Binya Passes By" symbolizes "primeval innocence, an unconcern with the passing of time and events, an affinity with the forests and mountains; this made her special and magical" (77). Through his love for Binya, the narrator realizes that in the mountains the niceties of "civilized" society—such as differences in education, culture, and age, and the social proprieties of staying within one's class, race, and economic boundaries—are of no consequence. Yet even in this romantic idyll there is opposition. Binya disappears one day, and when he looks for her, he learns that she has gone to her mother's village a hundred miles away. Perhaps her domineering grandmother has found out about them.

It is the constraints of the family or society that spoil the innocence of the female. While the male in Bond's love stories is always loyal and steadfast, the female is fickle, immature, or susceptible to the social considerations of respectability, status, financial security, and social approval. "Love Is a Sad Song," written around 1973–74 while he was editing *Imprint*, is an exposé of the intricacies involved in arranging a marriage and the controls placed on men and women. Structured as a narration addressed to sixteen-year-old Sushila, the object of his love, the protagonist, an Anglo-Indian writer of about thirty, looks back on his unrequited love by recounting the details of her coming to the hills, their falling in love, and her womanlike response to his lovemaking. Although he does not blame her, he "sings" this sad song, consoling himself that "[r]emembered passion grows sweeter with the passing of time" (210). The lover's thoughts are also a triumphant declaration of his enduring love and her fickleness. The conflict centers around the opposing expectations of a love relationship versus a traditional arranged marriage. While the narrator believes that their mutual love should culminate in marriage, Dinesh, his roommate and uncle of Sushila, makes it clear that although they are in love, the marriage—if it is ever to take place—must have the semblance of being arranged. According to B. S. Naikar, the future course of their love affair is evidence of cultural differences, because the narrator "seems to be quite ignorant about the Indian, especially Hindu...tradition [which] does not attach much importance to love before marriage. The couple are expected to fall in love with each other only after marriage" (97).

In deference to tradition, the protagonist tries to win allies in Sushila's family, but the main hurdle is the grandmother, the head of the family. Given the Indian system of arranged marriages, it is essential to have a "respectable" family intercede on his behalf, which he does not have. His suit is rejected because of the vast age difference, Sushila's need to complete her studies, and the possibility of her changing her mind later. He once again makes a trip to Delhi to find out if Sushila will elope with him when she turns eighteen, since that is the age when she can assume personal autonomy. But her love has been corrupted. Even as she says yes to him, her younger brother (who has acted as go-between) warns that she might change her mind because she likes someone richer, an officer in a bank who owns a car. Sushila seems to have succumbed to social pressures—the bank manager represents social status, excitement, and freedom to move out of her traditional family. It is significant that this change in her feelings occurs in the city, because when she visited him and her uncle in the hills—in the midst of nature—she was spontaneous and free. He remembers when she bathed with him in the waterfall, she stood beside him "naked, caressed by sunlight and a soft breeze coming down the valley" (220).

It is easy to understand how the Sushila of "Love Is a Sad Song" transforms into her namesake of "Time Stops at Shamli." The adult Sushila has lost her youthful bouyancy, and she purposefully continues in her incompatible marriage, rejecting the narrator's proposal to live freely in love but outside the rules of society. The narrator of "Time Stops at Shamli" is cynical when he comments that women are more concerned with security than personal happiness.

> I had always considered it an admirable thing to break away from security and respectability. Of course it is easier for a man to do this, a man can look after himself, he can do without neighbours and the approval of the local society. A woman, I reasoned, would do anything for love provided it was not at the price of security; for a woman loves security as much as a man loves independence. (57)

Haider considers the older, married Sushila of "Time Stops at Shamli" to be "the liberated woman, free from compunctions and taboos" (129), because she is willing to indulge in an extramarital affair with the protagonist when he comes to Shamli. Actually, she too is hedged in by society, by what people will say, and by financial security—love is not enough for her.

"Love Is a Sad Song" is based on an affair the author had with Anil Chopra's cousin, Sashi Kishore, and his frustrations with trying to arrange his marriage to her. The Kishore family did not take Bond seriously when he expressed interest in marrying Sashi, who was seventeen at that time. Because of the difference in their ages, they thought he was joking each time he broached the subject. Perhaps, if he had had a family to conduct the marriage negotiations for him, he would have been taken more seriously. After that, Bond was romantically involved with a couple of women, but he has remained a bachelor. Looking back on his life, he says that it was all for the best. "The breakup of my parents' marriage could have made me always turn back or made me hesitant to take that final knoll, in my view, that irrevocable step into marriage. Because my half-brothers and brother did get married, and they also had broken marriages" (Interview).

Bond's most controversial story is "The Sensualist: A Cautionary Tale," which was first serialized in *Debonair* (Bombay) in 1974 and then, after a gap of twenty-one years, was reprinted by Penguin Books India in an omnibus volume devoted to Bond's work. Structured as a story within a story, the two first-person narratives enable the author to present a debate between mind and matter, between unbridled enjoyment of sensual pleasures and total abstinence or renunciation of the world. A recluse narrates the story of his life to a traveler-pilgrim, telling how he used his overcharged sex drive to conquer and hold power over women. However, when a hill woman sexually overpowers him, he becomes impotent. Humiliated that an unlettered, ugly, hill woman has violated him, he decides to search for the truth by becoming an ascetic. He "removes himself from the scene of all physical activity" because, he reasons, "[i]t is useless to struggle against one's nature" (105). Bond once again touches on the conflict between city/civilization and the "overpowering innocence of the mountains" (134). The reclusive ascetic recognizes that as a rich, sophisticated city person he could appease his sensual hunger with a "civilized" veneer, while the hill woman was innocently gratifying her basic sexual desires. Unlike him, she is not scheming, yet she "stripped me of my manhood and pretensions" (133–34). The pilgrim sees this situation as sick and unhealthy because the recluse is hiding from the world and his true nature. The ascetic admits that he has overpowered his need for *kama* or material pleasures (food, drink, clothing, physical comforts, sex) by taking a weed that helps him to indulge in sensual pleasures through fantasy, without involving his body. The pilgrim argues that the ascetic has not renounced sensual pleasures but is running away from them; it is "a victory of matter over mind. Surely the only victory comes when the mind is free" (143). The ascetic's cave, then, is not the abode of a person who has attained peace but a place of dark hidden secrets, of the "cold ashes of his dead fire, and the cold corpse he still inhabits" (143).

The story can also be interpreted according to Carl Jung's theory of archetypes. The pilgrim is the hero on a quest to discover his true identity. He is lost on a dry mountain range, until he meets the ascetic. But the ascetic, instead of being a teacher or tutelary figure, turns out to be his unconscious personality, his shadow, an external embodiment of his unrecognized sins or excesses. Since there can be no real inner growth without confronting one's shadow, the pilgrim's discussion with the ascetic can be seen as his struggle to come to terms with his own sexual impulses and moral aberrations. He realizes that he cannot hide like an ascetic, and hence he wants to meet the hill woman in order to discover his manhood, his identity. The pilgrim's journey ends with: "I leave my dead self in the cave and continue my search for the perfect stranger in the night" (143).

In the introduction to *Strangers in the Night: Two Novellas*, Bond calls this novella a brooding, pessimistic piece, which is alien to his nature (xii). Written at a difficult time in the author's life, it led to further complications for him. A policeman came from a Bombay court with a nonbailable warrant for his arrest on the charge that this story was obscene. Accompanied by Prem Singh, Bond went to the local police station. Fortunately, a Mussoorie SDM (Sub-Divisional Magistrate) took the initiative to grant him bail, but the author had to appear in a Bombay court. He pleaded Not Guilty, and the case dragged on for about two years (the public prosecutor died in the meantime). Many writers testified in his behalf, and *Debonair* put up a strong defense until the judge acquitted Bond of the criminal charge of obscenity. Putting the event in perspective, Bond recognizes that he was a victim of the political atmosphere during the National Emergency declared by Prime Minister Indira Gandhi in 1975, when free speech was curtailed and many journalists and authors were persecuted (see Introduction, *Strangers* x–xi). Anyone who considers the story obscene has read it without understanding its moralistic theme. While the sexual exploits of the ascetic are listed quite frankly, the account is not sexually graphic in any way. It is more a psychological analysis and philosophical debate than a piece of fiction.

LONGING FOR THE PAST

Since moving to Mussoorie, Bond has fulfilled his dream of becoming a full-time writer and has established the direction of his personal life. It was a lonely and difficult journey, yet he has endured and succeeded. Bond, whose writings had always reflected a love and keen knowledge of the natural world, now established his identity as a personal nature writer. The subjects he writes about are somehow inextricably connected with nature. But, above all, his essays, short stories, and travel articles reflect his nostalgia for the past. Whether he is writing about small-town characters, the leisurely lifestyle of his childhood, or long-lost loves, it is the past he is celebrating.

Bond's emotional attachment to the past and his yearning to bring it back, if only by imaginatively re-creating it in his fiction, is related to his personal sense of loss. His one regret in life, he states in the introduction to *When Darkness Falls*, is that his father "was snatched away while I was still a boy," and that he was not able to spend more time with him (xi). In addition, when he returned to Dehra in 1955 from London, he was dismayed by the changes that modernization and the post-Independence era had brought to this small "garden town" of his childhood. Tongas were being replaced by scooter rickshaws and taxis, the bazaars were more crowded, new buildings were going up to accommodate the growing population, the houses of the British had been bought by Indian government and army officials, and tigers and wildlife had dwindled or become nearly extinct. Stories like "My Father's Trees in Dehra" and "The Last Tonga Ride" are a fictional account of the happy times he shared with his father, the old friendships, the joy of living in his grandmother's house, and his affinity for the banyan tree that was a place of refuge for him ("I removed my shoes and socks as people do when they enter a holy place" ["Last Tonga" 51]).

Yet Bond emphasizes that he is not being nostalgic in these stories, because "the only trouble with nostalgia is that one is inclined to gloss over the less pleasant parts of one's personal history," whereas he has tried to portray "both the positive and negative aspects" (Interview). Not everything in his past or the past of Dehra was happy or good—the divorce of his parents, his father's early death, World War II, communal riots that disturbed the peace of Dehra in 1947, psychological damage caused by displacement during Partition, and the expatriation of most Anglo-Indians, including nearly all his family members, who sold their homes and left for England. However, Bond does not dwell on these painful experiences. For instance, instead of focusing on the horrors of war, "Escape from Java" describes the close friendship between the nine-year-old British narrator and his Javanese friend. It develops the themes of interracial friendship, the senselessness of war, and the unconditional love of a father for his son. Through his stories, Bond also comes to terms with what was unpleasant in the past. In "The Last Time I Saw Delhi," he resolves the traumatic childhood experience of his parents' divorce. First published in the late 1980s in *Illustrated Weekly*, the story is based on notes the author had taken when he visited his mother in the hospital before her operation for breast cancer. The account is really a farewell to his mother and an acknowledgment that she taught him to have fun occasionally: "sometimes it is easier to tell the truth by disguising it as 'fiction'—especially when the subject is a painful one" (*Lamp* x).

Reminders of what was good in the past endure in the present—"treasures" left behind in a hole in the jackfruit tree are still there for the middle-aged protagonist of "When You Can't Climb Trees Any More" to retrieve after an absence of twenty-five years; the bungalow his grandfather built still stands; the mountains, river, and canals are still there; and the graves are lonely relics of the lives of Anglo-Indians. Above all, it is the trees that ensure continuity; Dehra is "one part of the world where trees are a match for man" (138), says the narrator of "My Father's Trees in Dehra." When he visits the dry riverbed where he and his father had planted trees just before his father's death, "the trees seem to know [him]. They whisper among themselves and beckon [him] nearer" (146). The trees also symbolize the permanence of his father's presence in Dehra. According to Satish C. Aikant, "It is this consolation in what remains that sustains the writer's faith, which otherwise would have made him cynical" (27).

Apart from these physical symbols of the past, memory is the real bridge that links the events of the past to the present. In "My Father's Trees in Dehra," the old street vendor remembers the history of the town, when the narrator's grandfather's house was built, what the family bought from him, and the grandchildren's visits. Similarly, in "As Time Goes By," past and present blend as the narrator (Bond) watches Prem Singh's boys and remembers his own friendship with Somi and Daljeet in the Dehra of his childhood.

> They did not see me, and I kept in the shadow of the trees and watched them play. But I didn't really see them. I was seeing Somi and Daljeet and the lazy old buffaloes, and I stood there for almost an hour, a disembodied spirit, romping again in the shallows of our secret pool. Nothing had really changed. Time is like that. (82)

NOTES

1. For additional information on Ruskin Bond's life in Mussoorie and Landour, refer to his autobiographical *Rain in the Mountains: Notes from the Himalayas*.

2. A copy of Ruskin Bond's current Will is included in his archival papers at Mugar Memorial Library, Boston University. Prem Singh and his family are his sole heirs.

3. A shortened version of "Sita and the River" was published as the children's book *Angry River*. The original story, intended for a general audience, was eventually published in *Collected Fiction*.

4. One notable exception is Dhan Gopal Mukerji, who lovingly recalls the grandeur and spiritual power of the Himalayas in novels like *Gay Neck: The Story of a Pigeon*, winner of the 1928 Newbery Medal.

5. This story was also written as a thirty-minute play for radio, entitled "It Must Be the Mountains," which was never broadcast or published until it was

included in *Rain in the Mountains*. In the radio version (like "Prospect of Flowers," written in the early 1970s), the story does not end unhappily with the death of the elderly protagonist. The author explains in a footnote to the play that the characters are based on Miss Ripley-Bean, who shared Maplewood Lodge with him for a short time; his friend Anil Chopra from Delhi; and 82-year-old Sir Edmund Gibson, once the British Resident of Kathiawar State, who spent his summers in Mussoorie after retirement.

6. Bond has developed this short story into the novella "Who Killed the Rani?" which is included in *A Season of Ghosts*.

WORKS CITED

Aikant, Satish C. "Reflections on a Bygone Era." *The Doon City Chronicle* [Dehra Dun] July 1997: 27–28.

Bond, Ruskin. *Angry River*. London: Hamish Hamilton, 1972.

___. "As Time Goes By." Bond, *Our Trees* 79–82.

___. "Binya Passes By." Bond, *Our Trees* 70–78.

___. "A Case for Inspector Lal." Bond, *Night Train* 16–21.

___. *Collected Fiction*. New Delhi: Penguin, 1999.

___. "Death of a Familiar." Bond, *Night Train* 88–100.

___. "Escape from Java." Bond, *Our Trees* 1–16.

___. *The Eyes of the Eagle*. London: Julia MacRae, 1987.

___. *Friends in Small Places: Ruskin Bond's Unforgettable People*. New Delhi: Penguin, 2000.

___. "From Small Beginnings." Bond, *Our Trees* 83–92.

___. *Ganga Descends*. Dehra Dun: English Book Depot, 1992.

___. "Ganga Descends." Bond, *Ganga Descends* 61–67.

___. "The Garlands on His Brow." Bond, *Night Train* 79–82.

___. "The Girl from Copenhagen." Bond, *Collected Fiction* 498–502.

___. "Great Trees of Garhwal." Bond, *Ganga Descends* 69–73.

___. Interview with Meena Khorana. Mussoorie, July 1995.

___. Introduction. Bond, *Our Trees* ix–xi.

___. "It Must Be the Mountains." Bond, *Rain* 6–77.

___. "A Job Well Done." Bond, *Night Train* 124–28.

___. "The Kitemaker." Bond, *Night Train* 101–04.

___. *The Lamp Is Lit: Leaves from a Journal.* New Delhi: Penguin, 1998.

___. "The Last Time I Saw Delhi." Bond, *Our Trees* 63–66.

___. "The Last Tonga Ride." Bond, *Our Trees* 48–58.

___. "Love Is a Sad Song." Bond, *Night Train* 210–37.

___. "The Magic of Tungnath." Bond, *Ganga Descends* 43–48.

___. "Most Beautiful." Bond, *Time Stops* 67–73.

___. *Mussoorie and Landour: Days of Wine and Roses*. Illus. Ganesh Saili. New Delhi: Lustre, 1992.

___. "My Father's Trees in Dehra." Bond, *Night Train* 138–46.

___. *The Night Train at Deoli and Other Stories*. New Delhi: Penguin, 1988.

___. *Our Trees Still Grow in Dehra*. New Delhi: Penguin, 1991.
___. *Panther's Moon*. New York: Random, 1969.
___. "The Prospect of Flowers." Bond, *Night Train* 110–15.
___. *Rain in the Mountains: Notes from the Himalayas*. New Delhi: Viking/Penguin, 1993.
___. "The Sensualist: A Cautionary Tale." Bond, *Strangers* 81–143.
___. "Sita and the River." Bond, *Collected Fiction* 153–86.
___. *Strange Men, Strange Places*. New Delhi: Rupa, 1992.
___. *Strangers in the Night: Two Novellas*. New Delhi: Penguin, 1996.
___. "Time Stops at Shamli." Bond, *Time Stops* 35–66.
___. *Time Stops at Shamli and Other Stories*. New Delhi: Penguin, 1989.
___. "A Village in Garhwal." Bond, *Ganga Descends* 13–20.
___. *When Darkness Falls and Other Stories*. New Delhi: Penguin, 2001.
___. "When You Can't Climb Trees Any More." Bond, *Night Train* 238–41.
___. "Who Killed the Rani?" *A Season of Ghosts*. By Bond. New Delhi: Viking, 1999. 93–210.
___. "The Writer on the Hill." Bond, *Ganga Descends* 1–4.
Dutta, Priyadarsi. "The God-Souled Himalayas." *The Hindustan Times* [New Delhi] 9 June 1999: 12.
Greenberger, Allen J. *The British Image of India: A Study in the Literature of Imperialism 1880–1960*. London: Oxford UP, 1969.
Haider, Aijaz. "The Woman in Bond's Short Stories." Singh 125–31.
Khorana, Meena G. "The River Is Eternal: Nature Mysticism and Vedanta Philosophy in Ruskin Bond's *Angry River*." *The Lion and the Unicorn* 19.2 (Dec. 1995): 253–68.
Khorana, Rohini. "Meeting Mr. Bond." *Shankar's Children's Art Number*. Ed. Yamuna Shankar. Vol. 44. New Delhi: Indraprastha (CBT), 1994. 57, 60.
MacMillan, Margaret. *Women of the Raj*. New York: Thames and Hudson, 1988.
Mukerji, Dhan Gopal. *Gay Neck: The Story of a Pigeon*. New York: Dutton, 1927.
Naikar, B. S. "The Paradox of Love in *Love Is a Sad Song*." Singh 96–99.
Singh, Prabhat K., ed. *The Creative Contours of Ruskin Bond: An Anthology of Critical Writings*. New Delhi: Pencraft, 1995.
Torgovnick, Marianna. *Gone Primitive: Savage Intellects, Modern Lives*. Chicago and London: U of Chicago P, 1990.

6

A Long Summer Afternoon: The Charmed World of Childhood

Ruskin Bond had already achieved recognition as a writer for adults before he turned to writing for children. Consequently, some of the major themes, events, and images that appear in his adult works also find their way into his children's stories. In his introduction to *The Night Train at Deoli and Other Stories*, he says that in the 1970s, when he was burdened by personal and professional problems, writing for children helped him out of his difficulties (no pag.). Prior to that, he had published an occasional short story for children in magazines and newspapers in India and abroad, but it was in Mussoorie, especially after moving to Ivy Cottage, that he started to write regularly for children. As a grandfather to Prem Singh's children, he was constantly inventing stories to amuse Rakesh, Mukesh, and Savitri, often making the children the protagonists. Writing children's stories also became a means by which Bond vicariously fulfilled his own needs and longings as a child, refashioning his unhappy and disrupted childhood into a secure and joyous time. He writes in *Scenes from a Writer's Life* that "I don't suppose I would have written so much about childhood or even about other children if my own childhood had been all happiness and light" (4). The introduction to *The Night Train at Deoli* also outlines Bond's approach to writing for children:

> In writing for children one has to adopt a less subjective approach; things must happen, for boys and girls have no time for mood pieces. So this kind of writing does help me to get away from myself. At the same time, because I have so strong an empathy with children, I can enter into their minds when I am writing about them. As children we are all individualists; it is only as we grow older that we acquire a certain grey similarity to each other. (No pag.)

Bond started writing for children during the postcolonial, post-Independence period when most Indian authors were producing didactic works to teach moral lessons or infuse national pride. However, Bond focused on entertaining young readers, recognizing their "innate wisdom and the thousands of years of civilization in their genes, but with all the freshness of a new life, a new day" (*Scenes* 90)—and in that lay his popularity and originality. His stories for children brought freshness, imagination, and, because of his Anglo-Indian background, a multicultural identity to Indian children's literature.

DEVELOPMENT OF INDIAN CHILDREN'S LITERATURE

At the time of Independence in 1947, there were no publishing houses that produced only children's books, and the adult publishers could not afford to invest in children's trade books. During the early post-Independence period, the most urgent need was to publish textbooks and supplementary readers to counteract the effects of colonialism and to replace the imported books used in schools where the medium of instruction was English. The National Council of Educational Research and Training (NCERT), a government organization, was established in 1961 to publish bias-free and appropriate textbooks and supplementary reading materials. However, the small English-speaking urban population had to continue relying on books and magazines imported from England and the United States for their leisure reading.

While India has a rich heritage of oral literature, the concept of a modern, creative children's literature written specifically with young readers in mind began only in the nineteenth century with exposure to Western education, imported books, introduction of the printing press, and the publications of Christian missionaries. According to Manorama Jafa, secretary general of the Association of Writers and Illustrators for Children, "[c]ontact with the West and the English language also introduced the concept of childhood and gave an impetus to the growth and development of literature for children as a separate discipline…books specially prepared for children began to appear with the establishment of the School Book Society, Calcutta, in 1817" ("From Goddess" 9). However, before the twentieth century, children's literature was mainly limited to retellings of traditional tales, adapting adult books for children, and translating foreign classics into Indian languages.

Until a viable publishing industry for children could be established, children's magazines in the major Indian languages and English provided the main avenue for established and new writers to contribute to the development of genres and the evolution of an "Indian" identity in children's literature. For those writing in English, the children's section of the Sunday editions of some of the leading English-language newspapers provided yet another forum. However, the authors focused on folktales, epics, and historical legends to convey the traditional heritage; biographies of past heroes and freedom fighters to infuse pride and provide role models; and realistic stories urging readers to be instruments of change in rebuilding the country.

Ironically, in spite of the country's nationalistic goals, English-language publishing was the first to develop. Because of India's multilingual, multiethnic population, English and Hindi served as link languages. The establishment of Children's Book Trust (CBT; New Delhi) in 1957 marks the beginning of modern Indian children's literature. Founded by Shankar Pillai, a political cartoonist, this private enterprise publishes exclusively for children. Its first two titles for children were published in 1961. Most of the early titles published by CBT were in English, and later some were translated into the major Indian languages, using the same illustrations and format. According to Jafa, CBT was a trendsetter, because the "quality of writing, art work, book design, printing and binding was better than books published by any other Indian publisher" ("Indian Sub-Continent" 809). To encourage the development of children's literature, CBT hosts training workshops for authors, organizes annual writing competitions, and promotes children's books through book fairs (Jafa, "Children's Literature" 39–40).

Another milestone in the development of children's literature was the founding of India Book House (IBH) in 1951, which began as a distributing company for imported books. In 1967, IBH started publishing children's books with its Echo Series, and it established the Amar Chitra Katha comics to counter the demand for imported comics from England and the United States (Menon 28). The National Book Trust (established in 1957), an autonomous organization under the Ministry of Human Resources Development, has been publishing books for children since 1969. To promote national integration and to make outstanding works in the indigenous languages and in translations available to all Indian children, it started the Nehru Bal Pustakalaya and Aadan Pradan series, which produce books in English and twelve Indian languages, using a common text and illustrations (Srinivasan 36–37).

Today, there are only fifty publishers in India who publish exclusively for children in all languages. About 500 new titles are produced each year in all the languages put together (Rao 70), which is inadequate considering that there are over 100 million school children in India between the ages of 6 and 17 (Carus 455). Children's publishers operate under severe financial constraints: high production costs, multilingual publishing, low literacy rate, low parental purchasing power, and competition from imported books. English-speaking children, who generally belong to the upper-middle class, can easily afford to buy the more expensive imports. These problems are further compounded by the fact that India produces children's literature in English and fourteen Indian languages, hence the readership in the individual languages is limited (Khorana, Introduction xi–xiv).[1]

Other outstanding English-language publishers are Frank Brothers, HarperCollins, Hemkunt, Penguin Books, Publications Division (Ministry of Information and Broadcasting), Ratna Sagar, Rupa, Scholastic, Sterling, Thomson, and Vikas. Two dynamic presses that were founded in the 1990s are Tulika and Tara. English-language publishers "encourage creative and original writing much more than the publishers in Indian languages. Today 40 percent of the children's books are published in English" (Jafa, "Children's Literature" 39). Apart from Indian classic literature, retellings of folktales, tales from mythology and history, and translations of Western classics, creative works in English are mostly imitations of popular British boarding school stories or the formulaic Enid Blyton mystery and adventure series. Poile Sengupta complains that Indian children's literature is overburdened by its agenda:

> Our national book breeding institutions lay down "rules"; writers must...uphold the principles of national unity, national and personal integrity, regional and religious tolerance, secularism, international understanding and global harmony! What subsequently emerges from this unholy mixture, is a moral science-cum-civics lesson with a thin anaemic story-line, which our English reading children shudder away from. (141–42)

Sengupta further states that most writers in English steer away from realistic portrayals of psychological and social pressures by creating "an exclusive, grossly false and overfed world, a designer world" in their books (142). Thus, she concludes, much Indian writing in English offers only "samples of Third World imitations of what others do much better" (146).

Ruskin Bond is the leading Indian writer for children in English. When he started writing for children in the 1960s and early 1970s, children's publishing was still in its infancy in India. There was very little scope for publishing books, hence he was restricted to publishing short stories in children's magazines abroad—such as *Cricket* (USA), *The Christian Science Monitor* (USA), *Elizabethan* (UK), *Reader's Digest* (USA), *The Lady* (UK), and *Asia Magazine* (Hong Kong)—and in English-language magazines and newspapers in India—such as *Children's World, The Times of India*, *The Illustrated Weekly of India*, *Deccan Herald*, *Statesman*, and *Hindustan Standard.* From the very beginning, Bond resisted writing didactic stories with a social or political agenda in mind; instead, he wrote imaginative stories to entertain and amuse young readers. In this, he displayed profound empathy for the inner world of the child, because it was not until 1979, the Year of the Child, that Indian publishers, writers, and scholars began to pay serious attention to the psychological and emotional needs of the child.

THE JOYOUS WORLD OF CHILDHOOD

Bond's view of childhood is quite different from the harsh reality portrayed in his adolescent novels, where the protagonists are victims of adult failure, economic and social problems, or incompatible marriages. The fictive world of the child is a time of summer, a carefree age of mischief and fun. A long summer afternoon serves as a metaphor for the secure and happy world of childhood.[2] "Social distinctions among children are irrelevant in this mellow atmosphere: British and Indian, rich and poor, Christian and Hindu, brahmin and low-caste mingle as equals" (Khorana, "Ruskin" 9). This view of childhood as a "charmed" time is eloquently captured in *Once upon a Monsoon Time* and "The Room of Many Colours," as discussed in Chapter 1.

Bond's idyllic attitude toward childhood was strongly influenced by his teenage reading of the British Romantic poets; simple, evocative poetry of Rabindranath Tagore; social realism of Mulk Raj Anand; and depiction of an Indian childhood in R. K. Narayan's *Swami and Friends* and Sudhin Ghose's *And Gazelles Leaping*. He shares Wordsworth's Romantic view that nature has a beneficent and formative effect on people who live in its midst, and Tagore's nostalgic rendering of childhood as an unspoiled and magical time. He sees dignity in the daily experiences and in the unpretentious lifestyle of the people who live in the small Himalayan towns and villages.

Bond's early stories for children, written in Delhi when he was in his twenties, re-create his Anglo-Indian childhood and the people and places he knew while growing up. The plots focus on journeys, friendships, and the simple pleasures and games of children. His first book for children, *The Hidden Pool*, a collection of short stories that he had published earlier, was brought out by the newly founded CBT. It is the story of a cross-cultural friendship between fifteen-year-old Laurie, the son of a British engineer in India (who is really the author as a boy), and his Indian friends Anil and Kamal, who introduce him to the festivals, foods, and folktales of India. Laurie's discovery of a hidden pool in the mountains seals their friendship—it is the place where they swim, wrestle, and make plans to trek up to a glacier at 12,000 feet above sea level. Their journey serves as an initiation rite that builds self-confidence and a love and respect for the Himalayas.

By the time Bond's second children's book, *Grandfather's Private Zoo*, was published by India Book House in 1967, he was already recognized as "one of India's best-loved story-tellers" (back cover). It is a collection of ten short stories that had been published previously in a variety of magazines and newspapers, some written in the early 1960s in Delhi and the remaining in Mussoorie. The collection is based on the happy times Bond had spent as a child at his grandmother's house in Dehra, and the accounts he had heard of his Grandfather Clerke's fondness for unusual house pets. To bring unity and coherence to the individual stories—and to appeal to young readers—the author presents the book as an autobiography, deliberately blurring the boundaries between the facts of his life and the details that he invents, hence making the preface a part of the fictional world he creates. The protagonist is an only child who comes to live with his grandparents in Dehra because his parents are abroad. He has an especially close relationship with his grandfather—the champion of wounded, sickly, or starving animals—who sneaks an array of unusual animals into the house—such as Toto, the monkey, who loves hot baths; the conceited python who loves to admire himself in the mirror; Harold, the hornbill, who bounces tennis balls; and Caesar, the crow, who rips everything to shreds. The lively antics of these animals, and the consternation they cause Grandmother and their relatives and neighbors, are narrated with whimsical humor. Grandfather appears to be eccentric but it is because he respects the rights of animals. Caring for his grandfather's menagerie instills in the narrator a gentleness and respect for animals and nature. The two are almost co-conspirators as they thwart Grandmother's efforts to get rid of the animals. While Grandmother appears to be the antagonist, because the animals disrupt her orderly household, she tolerates them and on occasion even nurses them back to health.

The narrator's sympathy for nature extends beyond the walls of the house to include the banyan tree in the garden and the muddy pond behind the house. Both places are natural havens that sustain a diversity of life. His friendship with Ramu, the farmer's son who comes to the pond with his buffaloes, helps him to bridge social barriers. He learns that although Grandfather and Ramu belong to different religions and cultures, both share the conviction that one should be gentle toward animals and not kill them. In the last story, "A Photograph," the protagonist finds an old photograph that reveals a different side of Grandmother. Although Grandmother does not admit it is her childhood picture, he recognizes the defiant body language and the devilish smile to be hers. Grandmother says that the girl was wicked, because she refused to be confined to her narrow Anglo-Indian world but would sneak off into the bazaar to eat Indian snacks, would refuse to dress in conventional clothing, and would swim in the canal like a tomboy. The protagonist learns just as much about freedom, enjoyment of nature, and not following conventions blindly from Grandmother as from Grandfather. *The Hidden Pool* and *Grandfather's Private Zoo* set forth all the important themes that will ripple through Bond's future works for children: duality of nature, conservation of animals, importance of trees, and cross-cultural friendships.

"A Tiger in the House" is another one of Bond's whimsical animal stories. Here Grandfather adopts a tiger cub, Timothy, who behaves just like a house pet. When Timothy starts to become unmanageable on a leash, he is presented to a zoo. Six months later, when Grandfather goes to visit the tiger, he puts his hand in the cage to tickle and pet the tiger and he even smacks him on the face, as in the past, when he growls. The zookeeper comes rushing to warn Grandfather that his tiger has died and that the one in the cage is a dangerous beast that was caught the previous month. Nevertheless, Grandfather still calls him Timothy and bids him goodnight. Obviously Grandfather speaks the tiger's language and has developed a rapport with him. This "Grandfather" story has a long printing history. Entitled "The Day Grandfather Tickled a Tiger," it was written around the same time as the stories in *Grandfather's Private Zoo*, and was published in the *National Observer* in the late 1960s and in *Cricket* in the early 1970s. The story has appeared in a number of anthologies, such as *Animals You Will Never Forget*, and it has been used in the New York State and Pennsylvania school examinations as a comprehension passage (Bond, Telephone conversation).

In Bond's animal stories, snakes, monkeys, and tigers come close only to those people who have empathy with nature and will not harm them. According to Deepa Agarwal, Bond's animal stories reflect an Anglo-Indian sensibility: "While Hindus may venerate cows and worship snakes, the Indian attitude to animals remains quite different—animals are not considered pets, but rather either loyal helpers or sacred objects, or both" (33). Bond does not anthropomorphize animals or write animal fantasies; rather, he sees animals as having feelings and rights on earth. Commenting on A. A. Milne's animal fantasies, which he had read as a child, Bond states: "Toy animals voicing human sentiments never did fascinate me. Appealing though animals may be as pets or in the wild, their civilization is different from ours. A better one, possibly; but distinct from ours" (*Scenes* 38).

During this early period in the development of Indian children's literature, Bond says "there were just a handful of us writing for children, often for little or no financial reward" ("To the Editor" 4). Indian publishers did not pay much, and since he was a full-time writer, he had to look abroad to publish his children's stories. In addition to children's magazines in India (*Children's World*, *Target*), England, and the United States, he published over twenty-five stories in *School Magazine* (Australia), published by the Department of Education (Sydney, NSW); and in the children's magazine in the Saturday issue of *Khaleej Time* (Young Time; Dubai). *Panther's Moon* and *Angry River*, both discussed in the next chapter, were his first children's books to be published abroad. However, it was *Angry River* that marked Bond's transition from an adult to a children's writer, and he considers it his "first and probably best children's novel" (qtd. in Chatterjee 7). Bond would spend the next two decades writing mainly for children.

In his thirties, Bond extended his vision of childhood as an age of pranks and fun to include other Indian children. Some of the stories in *The Road to the Bazaar* (first published in London in 1980) had first appeared in magazines; when compiling them in book form, Bond wrote two or three new stories and revised the original ones to give them one locale, common characters, and a developing relationship among the characters from story to story. The 1980 edition contained eleven stories, but with the new stories about Mukesh and Koki included in the 1991 edition, the collection now has sixteen stories. The publisher's blurb to the Indian edition states: "Ruskin Bond not only brings to life a town in northern India capturing the scenery, the people, the atmosphere—but also shows that children are the same the world over" (back cover).

The stories in *The Road to the Bazaar* focus on the friendships, quarrels, and simple fears and triumphs of a group of boys and one girl (Koki) who live in a small town that resembles the Dehra of Bond's childhood. "The timeless, magical atmosphere of the hill station in summer or during vacation quickly envelops [the] stories" (Khorana, "Ruskin" 8). Summer conveys a mood of comfort, optimism, and joyousness. Butterflies and beetles hum lazily as the children explore the hills, forests, and river beds; climb guava and lichi trees; and take afternoon naps under shady trees. "Parents do not worry about the safety of their children, who roam freely without fear of violence or crime because people from the hills are quick to smile, hospitable, and trusting" (Khorana, "Ruskin" 8). In this genial atmosphere, Bond narrates the adventures of the protagonists with sensitivity and gentle irony. In "The Long Day," Suraj leaves home for the whole day because he fears the postman is going to bring his failing report card, only to find out that reports are due the next day; and in "The Fight," when Anil refuses to give Vijay exclusive rights to swim in the forest pool just because he is stronger, the atmosphere gets ugly, but Vijay's childlike curiosity at Anil's ability to dive and swim underwater dissipates the tension and they become friends. Koki is a strong female character who frequently participates in the games as an equal—she defeats the boys in a beetle race and makes the winning catch in a cricket match.

Thirteen-year-old Suraj figures prominently in these stories. He senses the mystery of the world outside the small town and is fascinated by people who ride trains; he wants to visit new places, away from school and report cards. In "The Great Train Journey," he sneaks into an unlocked compartment of a goods train, thinking he is finally on his way to new and exciting places and will return home a hero. However, it turns out to be the local apple train, which, after stopping at a few small stations, brings him right back to his home town! In "The Tunnel," Suraj goes to the watchman's post to see the night train pass by. The jungle is safe; even the leopard who sleeps in the tunnel, which has to be shooed out by the watchman so that it won't be hit by the train, is not dangerous. Suraj enjoys the beauty and power of the train; it is the "beautiful dragon of his dreams" (8). But to the natural world, the train's intrusion is the one jarring note in the jungle's silence and peaceful harmony. The jungle seems to hold its breath, and then lives again only after the train has passed. It is this double vision that adds depth and force to the stories: the child's playful level and the thought-provoking philosophical level. Beneath the innocent and sheltered surface of the children's lives, there is a hint of adult problems or the presence of something potentially serious. For instance, Mohan, the poor vendor of knickknacks, tries to improve his job prospects by studying for the high school exam in his spare time, but he fails; and the boy Nathu causes a crisis for the local bank by declaring that he is not being paid regularly, but he is totally unaware of the trouble he has caused.

Bond's next collection of stories to be published in India was *The Adventures of Rusty*, set a couple of years before Independence. Structured in two parts, it recounts the experiences of young Rusty, a fictional character based on himself, who was first introduced in his adolescent novels *The Room on the Roof* and *Vagrants in the Valley*. Part I is a collection of six semiautobiographical stories set in Grandmother Clerke's home in Dehra. It gives a poignant portrait of the difficulties many Anglo-Indians faced at that time. Granny has to sell homemade pickles and chutneys to augment the small Railway pension of her late husband. Even though her daughters and their families want to move to England, Granny feels she has taken root in India, like the trees—and Rusty wants to stay back to look after her. The focus of this section, however, is on the hilarious misadventures of Uncle Ken, a nephew of Granny, who is handled with gentle irony as he makes feeble attempts to find a job—he tutors the maharajah's children, acts as tourist guide, and plays cricket. Through him, Bond deconstructs the image of the superior British sahib and pokes fun at the foibles and pretensions of this "uncolonial" Anglo-Indian. One laughs at Uncle Ken's eccentric behavior and sees through his laziness, but the portrait is not bitter or satirical because there is an underlying sympathy for someone who has not made anything of himself even though he is forty. The portrait of Uncle Ken is based on Kenneth Clerke, Bond's mother's half-brother, who lived by the philosophy that "the best way to go through life was to zigzag. In that way you saw more of the world and the world saw more of you!" (*Scenes* 71). Being the only brother in the midst of five doting sisters, he spent the year "zigzagging" through their homes, including Bond's mother's home. According to the author, Uncle Ken had immense plans for the future, but he never got around to putting them into action. After Independence, he moved to England, where one of his sisters had relocated. There he finally had to get a job—around the age of fifty—as a postman in a small village, and he was quite content delivering letters on a bicycle (Interview, 1995). The fictional character Uncle Ken (sometimes called Uncle Benji) makes brief appearances in several of Bond's stories.

While Part I contains individual episodes without an integral story line, Part II—Running Away—set a few years later, has a progressive, episodic plot. Rusty is an adolescent now, his parents have died, and he is under the charge of a guardian whom he hates. Rusty and his friend Daljit plan to run away from boarding school because they feel trapped and want to escape from school to pursue their dreams—Rusty of becoming a writer and Daljit of helping in his father's business in Kenya. They head for Jamnagar, 800 miles away, from where they hope to sail in Uncle Jim's ship to exciting, far-off places. They have many thrilling adventures en route: they come face to face with a tiger while trekking down the mountains, dodge the teacher at the railway station, are captured by a band of dacoits ("armed robbers"), and ride a freight train. After all this trouble, they find the ship has sailed just minutes before they arrive. This escapade is to be taken in a lighthearted manner, because they are never in any serious trouble: one dacoit loosens the rope with which they are tied so that they can escape, Daljit's uncle takes them back to school, and the school does not expel them. It is a story of friendship, of dreams. Bond does not describe Rusty's loneliness and pain at the loss of his parents or his miserable life with the hateful guardian, as he did in *The Room on the Roof*. Instead, the story ends on the philosophical note that dreaming of running away is an essential way of coping with life.

In the 1980s, many of the stories from the above collections were published as individual books by Julia MacRae Books (London) in its Blackbird and Redwing Series. Julia MacRae had published three books by Bond when she was managing editor for Hamish Hamilton's children's books. Bond continued to publish with her when she started her own company, first as a division of Franklin Watts, then with Walker Books, and a couple of years later as a division of Random Century (Interview, 1995). With one or two exceptions, most of these books are still in print.

Among the most interesting of these titles is *Cricket for the Crocodile*, which continues the story of Ranji, whom Bond had introduced in *The Road to the Bazaar*. Ranji loves to play cricket, a favorite sport and pastime inherited from the British but now very much a part of Indian life. Ranji's goal is to be a professional cricketer, so he does not miss a single opportunity to organize matches against the opposing village team. But the main challenge to the players comes from Nakoo, the crocodile, who lives in the river by the village. The perspective of Nakoo, a regular spectator at these matches, is an important one—he is disturbed by the noise and the cricket balls falling in the river, not to mention their frightening the creatures he wants for his meals. He tries to reclaim his territory by relaxing in the warm sun on the smooth cricket pitch, until one of the players hits him with a fast ball. He sulks and withdraws into the river, waiting to take revenge. As the run-by-run progress of the match is narrated, readers are also given the whereabouts and mood of the crocodile. The mounting tension of the game, and Ranji's dwindling hopes of winning the match, are humorously juxtaposed with Nakoo's plot to eat the bank manager, the father of a player on the town's team. When Nakoo slides under the string cot to await his opportunity, he does not notice the bank manager sleeping on top. Then a ball hits Nakoo on the jaw, and he furiously charges forth—but he is stuck under the cot! He knocks over cricket stumps, digs up the pitch, eats a glove and sun hat, and then makes for the river. The match is declared over—in a draw. So the crocodile actually helps Ranji's team! Although the crocodile poses a potential threat, the children are never in any danger because they respect the crocodile and stay away, and all Nakoo really wants is peace and quiet. The antics of the crocodile add comic relief to the seriousness with which the "friendly" match is being played.

Snake Trouble is an enhanced version of "The Conceited Python" that first appeared in *Grandfather's Private Zoo*. Interestingly, the Anglo-Indian protagonist of the Indian edition becomes Ranji in the British version. The tension in the story arises from Grandmother's efforts to get rid of the python and the snake's refusal to leave. The tongue-in-cheek humor further intensifies when Aunt Ruby comes to visit, and she thinks the python is deliberately trying to frighten her—in the guava tree, admiring himself in the mirror on her dressing table. The army major who lives next door is also upset when Ranji places the python in a basket in which Grandmother later decides to collect guavas to present to the major, who thinks she has played a joke on him. In retaliation, when the family takes a train journey to visit Aunt Ruby, he exchanges Grandmother's food hamper for one with another python in it. The python causes much commotion on the train and later at Aunt Ruby's. But all is in good humor, and no harm comes to anyone. The python is not a predator but a pet or accomplice to Grandfather and Ranji. It is a tribute to Bond's universality that even when the cultural setting is changed, the story is still relevant and meaningful. Barbara Walker's illustrations provide an authentic portrayal of the lifestyle of this well-to-do Indian family, details of the culture and clothing, and scenes on the railway platform and in the train.

ROLE OF ADULTS IN CHILDREN'S STORIES

A dominant theme in Bond's stories for younger children is that there is a loving, nurturing relationship between children and adults—not necessarily their parents. In very few stories does the protagonist have a nuclear family with a mother and father. When Bond does present a father, he is not necessarily a traditional father; he is emotional, caring, sensitive, and creative—no doubt reminiscent of Bond's father. His stories are critical of mothers who are either domineering or away at parties; yet he also portrays sweet, traditional mothers such as Somi's mother in *Vagrants in the Valley* or the woman in "The Woman on Platform 8." Mostly, parents either do not figure prominently in his stories or the child protagonist lives with grandparents or with some surrogate parent figure. No, his children are not wiser than the adults, and they do not challenge adult authority. Adults are figures that command respect; they pass on their wisdom to children and enable them to gain confidence and assume responsibilities. For example, in "Ranji's Wonderful Bat," Mr. Kumar, owner of the sports store, gives Ranji the bat with which he had scored a hundred runs in order to boost Ranji's confidence. He says: "A bat has magic only when the batsman has magic! What you needed was *confidence*, not a bat. And by believing in the bat, you got your confidence back!" (24). The author believes that the role of adult characters in his children's stories is "to protect in the first place, but also to provide companionship, and to some extent to guide and instruct, though this should not be done in a 'preachy' sort of way" (Interview, 1999).

As in *Grandfather's Private Zoo*, Bond's child protagonists often live with their grandparents. While the setting of this book is the author's Grandmother Clerke's home in Dehra, the only grandparent he knew, the protagonist's relationship with his grandfather is pure wish-fulfillment on the part of the author, because his grandmother was a practical person who did her duty by Ruskin but did not dote on him (see *Scenes* 34). Bond's stories of doting grandparents were inspired by his attachment to his adoptive grandchildren and his enjoyment in seeing Rakesh, Mukesh, and Savitri growing up in his home—and it is this wonder and joy of raising a child that constitutes the enduring charm of these stories. His grandparent–grandchild stories touchingly portray the warmth of intergenerational relationships, the passing of traditions from the old to the young, and the self-esteem that children develop when brought up in such a secure and loving environment.

"The Cherry Tree" was written for Rakesh, who was frail and sickly as a child and with whom Bond did much babysitting. The story likens the growth of the protagonist, Rakesh, to a cherry seed that he plants and cares for until it matures into a tree. Rakesh nurtures the plant through its difficult early life when a goat eats it and a woodcutter cuts it down. At first, the growth of the cherry tree and the boy are parallel, but the tree far surpasses Rakesh when in a few years it flowers and gives fruit. It eventually becomes an ecosystem with little communities growing around it—insects live in it, bees take its nectar, and birds peck at the blossoms, just as Rakesh and his grandfather rest under its shade. At the end of the story, Rakesh feels proud of the seed that he had planted and seen to maturity: "'I wonder,' he whispered, 'Is this what it feels to be God'" (137). Likewise, readers become aware of the love with which Grandfather is raising Rakesh. Like the tree, he has also grown taller and stronger and can help his father in the fields.

Regrettably, in the U.S. version—first published in *Highlights for Children* in 1988 and then as the picture book *Cherry Tree*—all references to this mystical connection between a child's growth and creation have been omitted. While this version retains the love between grandfather and grandchild (the granddaughter Rakhi in this case), it lacks depth and philosophical meaning. Allan Eitzen's illustrations are attractive and well executed, but they give the story the stereotypical rural setting that is usually projected in American children's books about India. They portray the grandfather as a villager instead of a retired forest ranger, as in the Indian text; and his cottage is pictured as a hut. Likewise, instead of sitting on furniture, the grandfather and Rakhi sit on the ground outside the house, even in the winter, huddled in front of a fire; and Rakhi does not wear a school uniform, with gum boots and raincoat, as Rakesh does in the Indian version. Basically, the illustrations promote the image of India as a poor country, and the adult character as an uneducated villager. In addition, the illustrations do not maintain the integrity and cultural authenticity of the Himalayan background; the grandfather's clothes, for example, appear to be exotic, belonging to a different region of the country.

Another book that evokes the loving relationship between grandparent and grandchild is *Getting Granny's Glasses*. In this story, Mani offers to accompany his grandmother on a two-day journey to Mussoorie, where the nearest eye hospital is located, so that she can get new glasses. The atmosphere of this Himalayan region during monsoons is charmingly described as the two set off on their adventure. They walk through fields and forests, up and down mountains, see a river rushing swiftly, pass a mule-driver singing a romantic song, and admire a flock of parrots and the hills "bathed in golden sunshine" (22). At the small market town of Nain, they board a rickety bus that will take them to Mussoorie. However, there's been a landslide, and Granny and Mani decide to take a short cut—a stiff ten miles uphill—to Mussoorie and its jostling crowds. The glasses renew Granny's zest for life, and she buys gifts for the whole family, including a bell for the cow. With her improved vision, Granny excitedly rediscovers the beauty of her surroundings, but her greatest joy is seeing what a fine boy Mani has grown up to be.

The Blue Umbrella (originally published by Hamish Hamilton in 1974) displays a complex adult-child relationship in which the worst in human nature comes out when the characters give in to greed or materialism. It is the story of ten-year-old Binya, a simple girl from the Garhwal region, who is fascinated by a city woman's frilly blue silk umbrella. It was "like a flower, a great blue flower that had sprung up on the dry brown hillside" (12). Binya ultimately trades her precious leopard-claw necklace—which the woman covets—for the umbrella, partly due to her childlike desire to own something pretty and partly because no one else in her village has such a beautiful umbrella: "It had cast a spell over her, drawing her forward almost against her will" (14–15). It casts the same spell over everyone in the village; some even try to buy one on their trip to the nearest town, but it is only available in a big city like Delhi. Binya takes the umbrella everywhere with her—to graze the cows, fetch water, and deliver milk—and everyone is in awe of it.

Although Binya is surrounded by the beauty of nature, the umbrella becomes a symbol of the attractions of the outside world that she may never get to see. While this acquisitiveness may be childlike and even charming in Binya, in Ram Bharosa, the owner of the village store, it unleashes an inordinate desire to own the umbrella. When Binya does not succumb to his pressure to sell it to him, his helper offers to steal it—but he is caught by Binya's brother. When the villagers learn of Ram Bharosa's dishonesty, they stop going to his shop and his business starts to fail. Binya realizes her responsibility in Ram Bharosa's downfall: "She couldn't help feeling that in a small way she was the cause of the sad look on Ram Bharosa's face...and the ruinous condition of his shop...she didn't want him to feel too bad about what he'd done, because it made her feel bad about herself" (75–76). Peace and harmony are restored to the village when Binya makes a gift of the umbrella to Ram Bharosa. This simple gesture leads to his regeneration, because he in turn shares the umbrella with all the villagers.

While the lesson that children must learn to share instead of flaunting their possessions is quite apparent, the story is not written in a didactic or moralistic tone. The author shows respect for the intelligence of children to discriminate between right and wrong and allows them to resolve their inner conflicts as they gain experience and understanding. Binya does some soul-searching: "But had she loved the umbrella too much? Had it mattered more to her than people mattered?" (75). Ironically, the umbrella brings out jealousy in everyone—children as well as adults. On the one hand, it represents the corrupting influence of the outside world—a recurring theme in Bond's stories—and on the other it emphasizes that this encounter leads to growth and self-knowledge for Binya and Ram Bharosa and to the recognition that villagers too have the need to own an aesthetically beautiful object.

OF PRINCES, GHOSTS, AND DEMONS

Bond is primarily a writer of realistic stories. He does not favor modern fantasy, but his interest in the improbable is explored through stories of ghosts and supernatural beings. Hence, there is an "unseen" or magical dimension even to some of his realistic stories. For example, the protagonist sees visions of his dead father when he is in need, or the ghost of Great-Aunt Lilian tucks in the author every time he throws off his blanket while sleeping. In the introduction to *The Penguin Book of Indian Ghost Stories*, a collection he edited for adults, Bond states that ghosts are not bound by time or physical barriers, because they are "intangibles" and "do not recognize our impermanent, man-made frontiers" (x). He enjoys writing ghost stories for adults and children, and nearly all his collections include a few samples. He says that he became addicted to reading ghost stories at the age of ten when he discovered M. R. James's *Ghost Stories of an Antiquary*, which was one of the books he found in the forest resthouse while on the hunting trip with his stepfather. And, of course, his father had told him Kipling's famous story of the phantom-rickshaw in Simla. The author confesses that he has never seen a ghost, but that as he gets older he finds himself "becoming more 'receptive' to the spirits of those who have left this world and may be living on another plane" (ix). Bond's psychological approach to the supernatural was influenced by American author Lafcadio Hearn (1850–1904), who wrote that "[t]he ghostly always represents some shadow of truth. The ghost story has always happened in our dreams and reminds us of forgotten experiences, imaginative and emotional" (qtd. in Introduction, *Time Stops* 10).

Several of Bond's stories are based on the legends about the ghosts of Anglo-Indians who still haunt the hill stations, "ghosts of soldiers, adventurers, engineers, magistrates, memsahibs, their children, even their dogs!" (*Mussoorie and Landour* 29). When he first came to live in Mussoorie, he heard many tales of hauntings from his neighbor Miss Ripley-Bean. She reported personally having seen ghosts of the people she had known, such as of her long-dead father, who would visit her to ask why she had sold the family home. Bond discusses the topic at length in *Mussoorie and Landour: Days of Wine and Roses*, stating that there are more ghosts of the British in India because they "were restless here, so far from the shores of their small green island. And being restless in life, it was only natural that they should remain restless in death" (29). With typical Bondian humor, he advances the theory that "a burial is not perhaps as final as a cremation. A Christian, interred complete in his parts, may well be tempted to resume his earthly form again!" (29). Yet it is not the cemetery that these ghosts haunt.

> After all, we are already dead (or ought to be) when we are placed in our graves, and our ghosts, if restless, are more likely to visit the places where they lived and breathed and had their being; an old home, a familiar bench. Or, if one has left the world in unhappy circumstances, one might want to revisit the scene of the tragedy to see, perhaps, if things cannot yet be set right. (28–29)

Since many of the houses that the British built in Mussoorie and Landour still stand, Bond is not surprised that the former residents would want to visit their homes! His best story about a haunted house is "Whispering in the Dark," where the narrator takes refuge in a deserted old house on a stormy night. The house turns out to be perfectly maintained by the ghosts of two Anglo-Indian sisters, one pretty and the other ugly, who used to lure rich elderly gentlemen into their boarding house, rob them, and then suffocate them. The eerie atmosphere of the haunted house and the spine-chilling account of the narrator's brief stay there are skillfully narrated—the mysterious whispers about how the victim should be treated, a kiss with death-cold lips, reflections of a spectral figure in the mirror, and his experience of being nearly suffocated with a pillow. "The Monkeys" is another story about a haunted house, except that the action takes place in the garden. The narrator, a recent tenant of the house, is awakened at night by the barking of the ghost dogs owned by the previous tenant, Miss Fairchild, who lived there fifteen years back. From his neighbor Colonel Fanshawe, he learns that Miss Fairchild's garden was often raided by a band of silver-grey "langoor" monkeys, who would destroy her prize dahlias. She shot one of them, disregarding the local belief that it is a bad omen to kill a monkey: "It's not only that they are sacred to Hindus—but they are rather human, you know" (20). The narrator then witnesses the ghostly reenactment of Miss Fairchild's death when the monkeys tear apart her body, while her dogs try frantically to save their mistress.

Bond is also familiar with Indian stories of various types of ghosts—stories of mischievous jinns who can elongate their arms at will; of ghosts who wait in peepal trees for unwary travelers; and of churels, whose feet always face backward. The Garhwal region is also rich in such folklore because, as he states in the novella "The Sensualist: A Cautionary Tale," the hill folk are susceptible to supernatural forces: "It has something to do with their fear of the dark, their belief in demons and malignant spirits who dwell in trees or take possession of the bodies of leopards and sometimes humans" (126). "Eyes of the Cat" was inspired by local legends of humans who transform into supernatural animals to mete out justice to their adversaries. In this story, Binya is hurt by the repeated insults of her insensitive teacher, so on a night of the full moon she transforms into a leopard and waits for "madam" to return from a night out at her ladies club. The teacher is promptly killed and dragged into the bushes. In her human form, Binya is too poor, weak, and bound by the respect due to elders to retaliate against the scorn of the teacher, but as a leopard she has the power to avenge herself.

Among his earliest ghost stories for children was the whimsical *Ghost Trouble*, published in book form by Julia MacRae, and later included in Philippa Pearce's anthology *Dread and Delight: A Century of Children's Ghost Stories*. Just as Grandfather and Ranji are willing to share their home with animals, they now extend the same tolerance and hospitality to a mischievous *pret* ("ghost") when the peepal tree he lives in outside the family's house is cut down by the city to widen the road. The ghost moves indoors and plays a lot of harmless pranks, but eventually the family agrees that the pret likes them and are reconciled to its presence in the house. However, not all ghosts are so entertaining. In the collection *A Season of Ghosts*, there are a variety of stories about ghosts, demons, and fairy creatures. In each, the ghost is not an evil being but its behavior is dependent upon his or her experiences while alive. In "Wilson's Bridge," the ghost of a wronged wife continues to jump off the bridge into the swirling waters of the river below; her husband, "Pahari" Wilson, comes riding a horse to save her, but he is too late. The ghost of the happy-go-lucky boy who died in a bicycle accident in "Whistling in the Dark" is nurturing and protective toward the protagonist. Like a guardian angel, he saves the protagonist's life one misty night when the mountain road collapses in a storm, and from then on he continues to watch over him. The most macabre story is "Night of the Millennium," about a poor widow who lives in a tomb in the cemetery with her brood of hungry children. She feeds her children on the flesh of the men who come to her for sexual gratification. The didactic treatment of this story is unmistakable. The victim is an overconfident, successful, and aggressive young man who wants to use the widow to display his power—and he gets his just reward.

In tracing the development of Bond's ghost stories, Champak Chatterji states that the influence of Lafcadio Hearn is evident in the later stories. His ghosts are now more human, she says: "The menace goes out of his ghosts to be replaced instead by a hunger for life—a pathetic yearning for inclusion and love" (144). This is evident in "Topaz," where the protagonist falls in love with the ghost of a young girl who committed suicide when her lover deserted her; and in "Picnic at Fox-Burn," where the ghosts of two Anglo-Indian children come to play near the ruins of their old house. While it is correct to state that the ghosts in many stories are "Trapped in the woof of time, imploring still" (xv), to quote from Bond's poem "Out of the Dark," his most recent collection of stories, *When Darkness Falls and Other Stories*, displays a range of ghost stories. It includes two stories of Anglo-Indian ghosts who long for their past lives ("The Ghost in the Garden" and "Return of the White Pigeon"); one story about a *munjia*, the ghost of a brahmin who dies on the eve of his marriage ("The Family Ghost"); and one story of a woman who caused the deaths of her seven husbands, and now her malignant spirit is looking for its final victim ("Susanna's Seven Husbands").

In addition to ghost stories, Bond has also published some of his favorite tales from the diverse oral tradition of India. To fulfill the demands of his grandchildren, he states in the introduction to *Tales and Legends from India* that he had to go "further back in time, to the young heroes and heroines, Gods and Demons, of myth, legend and folklore" (10). In *Tales and Legends*, a collection of twenty-five stories, the author conveys the multicultural richness and variety of Indian traditional literature by selecting stories from different racial and tribal groups, religions, and geographical regions. The tales range from historical legends of strength and valor; to stories in which simple characters outwit the "clever" and more powerful ones; to fairy tales with complicated quests, magical objects, and transformations. The Sanskrit epic *Ramayan* is the subject of *The Adventures of Rama and Sita* and *Hanuman to the Rescue*, where Bond narrates the story of the capture and rescue of Sita, the heroine.

Each story is organized around a strong plot that allows for interaction between characters and events, and the episodes are developed for their human interest and universal qualities. For instance, in "A Battle of Wits," a trickster tale included in another collection, *Tales Told at Twilight*, a clever psychological ploy is used to outsmart the village *bania* ("shopkeeper"), who thinks that Jat farmers are simple-minded. While going into town one day, the Bania and a Jat tell each other tall tales, with the agreement that whosoever does not believe the other's story will be the loser. The Jat tricks the Bania by inventing a story in which the Bania owes him money.

> This placed the Bania in a dilemma. He had admitted a debt before a third party. If he said that it was merely a story, and completely untrue, he would have to pay the Jat five hundred rupees according to the terms of the wager. If he said it was true, he would have to pay the amount to the *mahajan* ["moneylender"]. Either way he was the loser. (131)

The settings and characters come alive through telling details, lively dialogue, and narrative ease. The language is always simple yet lyrical, as is evident in "The Mountain Lake," a complicated story of a prince's quest, which begins with this engaging description:

> There were no stars in the sky, nor was there the moon, as Prince Safir, tired and footsore, trudged on towards the towering mountains, which never seemed to get nearer. In the mountains lay his journey's end, the land of his dreams, which he knew he must reach one day. (3)

Bond brings his skill as a writer to his narration of traditional stories, because he believes that the folktale is the "true ancestor of the modern short story" (Preface, *Tales Told* 2). He has also enriched this genre by recording the legends and folklore of the Anglo-Indians who sojourned briefly in the Garhwal region. It is significant that this oral tradition is rooted in the cultural and historical experiences of the past two centuries, whereas Bond's Indian tales belong to a more ancient time. Through these stories, Bond has established the literary archetype of the Anglo-Indian ghost, symbolic of the lives and activities of the British in India—and of their loss and loneliness when that life ended.

NOTES

1. Also refer to K. A. Jamuna, *Children's Literature in Indian Languages*.

2. I had briefly introduced this idea in my article "Ruskin Bond: In the Lap of the Himalayas."

WORKS CITED

Agarwal, Deepa. "Contemporary Indian Fiction in English: A Colonial Legacy." *Bookbird* 34.4 (Winter 1996): 32–34.

Bond, Ruskin. *The Adventures of Rama and Sita*. London: Julia MacRae, 1987.

___. *The Adventures of Rusty*. New Delhi: Thomson, 1981.

___. *Angry River*. London: Hamish Hamilton, 1972.

___. "A Battle of Wits." Bond, *Tales Told* 125–31.

___. *The Blue Umbrella*. Calcutta: Rupa, 1992.

___. "The Cherry Tree." Bond, *Night Train* 133–37.

___. *Cherry Tree*. Honesdale, PA: Caroline House, 1991.

___. "The Conceited Python." Bond, *Grandfather's* 10–19.

___. *Cricket for the Crocodile*. London: Julia MacRae, 1986.

___. "The Day Grandfather Tickled a Tiger." *Animals You Will Never Forget*. Pleasantville, NY: Reader's Digest, 1969. 202.

___. "Eyes of the Cat." Bond, *Panther's Moon and Other Stories* 57–59.

___. "The Family Ghost." Bond, *When Darkness* 86–91.

___. "The Fight." Bond, *Road* 47–55.

___. *Getting Granny's Glasses*. London: Julia MacRae, 1985.

___. "The Ghost in the Garden." Bond, *When Darkness* 28–35.

___. *Ghost Trouble*. London: Julia MacRae, 1989.

___. *Grandfather's Private Zoo*. Bombay: India Book House, 1967.

___. "The Great Train Journey." Bond, *Road* 108–15.

___. *Hanuman to the Rescue*. New Delhi: Rupa, 1993.

___. *The Hidden Pool*. New Delhi: Children's Book Trust, 1966.

___. Interview with Meena Khorana. Mussoorie, July 1995.

___. Interview with Meena Khorana. New Delhi, November 1999.

___. Introduction. Bond, *Time Stops* 9–10.

___. "The Long Day." Bond, *Road* 26–33.

___. "The Monkeys." Bond, *Panther's Moon and Other Stories* 17–22.

___. "The Mountain Lake." Bond, *Tales Told* 3–13.

___. *Mussoorie and Landour: Days of Wine and Roses*. New Delhi: Lustre, 1992.

___. "Night of the Millennium." Bond, *Season* 65–72.

___. *The Night Train at Deoli and Other Stories*. New Delhi: Penguin, 1988.

___. *Once upon a Monsoon Time*. Hyderabad: Orient Longman, 1974.

___. "Out of the Dark." Bond, *Penguin Book* xv–xvi.

___. *Panther's Moon*. New York: Random, 1969.

___. *Panther's Moon and Other Stories*. New Delhi: Puffin, 1991.

___. *The Penguin Book of Indian Ghost Stories*. Ed. Bond. New Delhi: Penguin, 1993.
___. "A Photograph." Bond, *Grandfather's* 81–90.
___. "Picnic at Fox-Burn." Bond, *Ruskin Bond's Treasury of Stories for Children*. New Delhi: Viking, 2000. 105–08.
___. Preface. Bond, *Tales Told* 1–2.
___. "Ranji's Wonderful Bat." Bond, *Road* 16–25.
___. "Return of the White Pigeon." Bond, *When Darkness* 36–38.
___. *The Road to the Bazaar*. Rev. and exp. ed. 1991. New Delhi: Rupa, 1993.
___. "The Room of Many Colours." *Time Stops at Shamli and Other Stories*. By Bond. New Delhi: Penguin, 1989. 15–34.
___. *The Room on the Roof*. London: André Deutsch, 1956.
___. *"The Room on the Roof" and "Vagrants in the Valley": Two Novels of Adolescence*. New Delhi: Penguin, 1993.
___. *Scenes from a Writer's Life: A Memoir*. New Delhi: Penguin, 1997.
___. *A Season of Ghosts*. New Delhi: Viking, 1999.
___. "The Sensualist: A Cautionary Tale." *Strangers in the Night: Two Novellas*. New Delhi: Penguin, 1996. 81–143.
___. *Snake Trouble*. London: Julia MacRae, 1990.
___. "Susanna's Seven Husbands." Bond, *When Darkness* 56–62.
___. *Tales and Legends from India*. New Delhi: Rupa, 1990.
___. *Tales Told at Twilight*. Bombay: India Book House, 1970.
___. Telephone conversation with Meena Khorana, January 2002.
___. "A Tiger in the House." Bond, *Time Stops* 154–57.
___. *Time Stops at Shamli and Other Stories*. New Delhi: Penguin, 1989.
___. "Topaz." Bond, *Penguin Book* 146–50.
___. "To the Editor." *Bookbird* 35.4 (Winter 1997): 4.
___. "The Tunnel." Bond, *Road* 1–9.
___. *When Darkness Falls and Other Stories*. New Delhi: Penguin, 2001.
___. "Whispering in the Dark." Bond, *Time Stops* 118–22.
___. "Whistling in the Dark." Bond, *Season* 1–10.
___. "Wilson's Bridge." Bond, *Season* 1–20.
___. "The Woman on Platform 8." Bond, *Night Train* 13–17.
Carus, Marianne. "Children's Magazines." Hunt 443–57.
Chatterjee, Manini. "The Other Bond." *Telegraph* [Calcutta] 8 Dec. 1991: 4–8.
Chatterji, Champak. "Bond and the Witching Hour." *The Creative Contours of Ruskin Bond: An Anthology of Critical Writings*. Ed. Prabhat K. Singh. New Delhi: Pencraft, 1995. 142–45.
Dasgupta, Amit, ed. *Telling Tales: Children's Literature in India*. New Delhi: Indian Council for Cultural Relations & New Age International/Wiley Eastern, 1995.
Hunt, Peter, ed., and Sheila Ray, associate ed. *International Companion Encyclopedia of Children's Literature*. London and New York: Routledge, 1996.
Jafa, Manorama. "Children's Literature in India." Dasgupta 33–42.

___. "From Goddess to Prime Minister: Changing Images of Women in Indian Children's Literature." *Bookbird* 34.1 (Spring 1996): 6–12.

___. "The Indian Sub-Continent." Hunt 807–22.

Jamuna, K. A. *Children's Literature in Indian Languages*. New Delhi: Publications Division, Ministry of Information and Broadcasting, 1982.

Khorana, Meena. Introduction. *The Indian Subcontinent in Literature for Children and Young Adults: An Annotated Bibliography of English-Language Books*. Westport, CT: Greenwood, 1991. Xi–xxxiv.

___. "Ruskin Bond: In the Lap of the Himalayas." *Writer and Illustrator* 12.2 (Jan.–Mar. 1993): 8–11.

Menon, Navin. "A Historical Survey." *Children's Literature in India*. Ed. Menon and Bhavana Nair. New Delhi: Children's Book Trust, 1999. 23–45.

Pearce, Philippa. *Dread and Delight: A Century of Children's Ghost Stories*. New York: Oxford UP, 1995.

Rao, Mohini. "Children's Books in India: An Overview." Dasgupta 67–73.

Sengupta, Poile. "Writing for Children in India in English." Dasgupta 141–46.

Srinivasan, Prema. *Children's Fiction in English in India: Trends and Motifs*. Chennai: T. R., 1998.

7

The Duality of Nature: Poems and Stories for Children

The world of the child, as we saw in the previous chapter, is a safe and benign one, where nature and humans exist in harmony. Nature's comforting presence in the lives of children is best captured in *To Live in Magic: A Book of Nature Poems*, *An Island of Trees: Nature Stories and Poems*, and *Granny's Tree Climbing and Other Poems*, a recent publication of Bond's best-known poems for children. *To Live in Magic*, a handsome collection of nature poems for younger children (now out of print), accompanied by Suddhasattwa Basu's exquisite illustrations, reveals Bond's philosophy that "[i]n everything is good, in everything is beauty" (qtd. in Note to Parents and Teachers). This theme is distilled to its essence in his simple lyrical verses, which are almost "prayers" to the various manifestations of nature—to each new sunrise and the beautiful night that follows, to old trees that bless the house with their shade, to foolish beetles without a sense of direction, to a lone fox dancing, and to a boy riding a mule on the rough mountain path. The poet reveres "silence" because then one can "listen" to the "summer grass singing," "dawn dew falling," "pebbles humming," and "the moon as it climbs the sky" ("Listen!" [15]). In nature, he finds the personal qualities to lead a meaningful life: a quiet and gentle voice to comfort others and a strong and upright demeanor like the chestnuts and pines, but also "To be humble like the willow, / Which bows low gracefully" ("Growing with Love" [21]). Bond acknowledges that life can have its "tumbles" and difficulties, but his prayer is "Let me find in me a rock to cling to" ("The Fern" [24]).

These uplifting poems will prompt young readers to contemplate the significance of the humblest aspect of nature.

While the poems in *To Live in Magic* are mainly observations of the beauty and mystery of nature, those in *An Island of Trees* celebrate a more direct interaction with nature. Whether it is the bat doing stunts under the furniture, a lullaby that encourages Rakesh not to be afraid of the big river or the dark night, the bravery of a snail for crossing the hazardous road to get his meal, or the owl's right to hoot in the night, each poem respects the unique qualities and differences of others and declares that we can all live in harmony by "not tak[ing] from any man his song" ("Lullaby" [23]). Above all, there is a symbiotic relationship between people and trees. In the title poem of *Granny's Tree Climbing*, an elderly grandmother is willing to "grow old disgracefully" but she cannot bear to give up her tree-climbing, because "Ever since childhood, she'd had this gift / For being happier in a tree than in a lift." Eventually, her son and grandson build her a tree-house, "Upholding her right to reside in a tree" ("Granny's Tree Climbing" [22, 23]). The author believes that trees have an enduring presence in our lives; they are our connection to the past, even in the midst of change.

> I listen to their whisperings,
> Their own mysterious diction;
> And bow my head before their arms
> And ask for benediction. ("The Trees," *Granny's Tree Climbing* 19)

Bond moves from this idyllic view of nature to a more realistic one in order to show that children are part of nature's battle for survival. He says: "I began with a rather romantic, pastoral image of childhood, but I became more realistic as time went by" (Interview). His child protagonists do not just revel in the glory of their natural surroundings; they face danger, natural disasters, or the death or illness of an adult caregiver. They go on adventures and solve mysteries, but not in the Enid Blyton-style that is so popular among Indian writers in English today. Nature is the antagonist in these stories, and the characters confront the threatening situations by using their intelligence and stored knowledge. Their adventures are associated with surviving floods, forest fires, earthquakes, or predators, and the mysteries they solve pertain to an understanding of their place in nature's universal scheme. Although not always articulated as such—since the perception is that of a child—their experiences also lead to maturity and an acceptance of the benign and destructive aspects of nature.

COSMIC DANCE OF THE UNIVERSE: AN ANALYSIS OF *ANGRY RIVER*

In his many poems, short stories, and novels for children, Ruskin Bond's characters come to a realization of their spiritual affinity with nature through a single manifestation of nature. Whether it is a cherry tree, a raindrop, a window on the roof from which to view the world, a hidden pool, or an old banyan tree, a single facet serves as a symbol of harmony with nature and a transcendental vision of life. In *Angry River*, the manifestation of nature is a river that tumbles down from the melting glaciers and snows of the high Himalayas.[1] Bond explores his protagonist's changing relationship with the river, from a deep love and gratitude for its many boons, to an awareness of its duality, to an understanding of its mystical nature.[2] Through this simple story Bond also reveals his deep insight into the philosophical concepts of Hindu scriptures and metaphysical thought.

As is typical of Bond's stories for children, *Angry River* is placed in an isolated, pretechnological setting whose inhabitants still retain their "inherited values of basic honesty, faith, and love for the family and neighbours" (Saraiya 3). The central action is focused on a small island in the middle of a big river with numerous villages dotting its banks. The river has no specific name; it is simply called "the river." An examination of Bond's papers, however, indicates that the location could be Rishikesh, a small town some thirty-five miles below Mussoorie, which he had visited in the late 1950s and described as follows: "The river (Ganges) emerges from the foothills with a low boom, swift and strong…" (Papers).

A timeless, magical atmosphere quickly envelops the island with its peepal tree in the center and a single mud hut built against a huge rock. For as long as ten-year-old Sita and her grandparents have been living there, the island and the teeming life that the river supports have been a microcosm of the world to the family. Their attitude toward the river that sweeps around their small world is both practical and reverent; they lovingly regard it as their provider. The river enables them to be self-sufficient by supplying their daily needs: water for their melons and vegetables, water for drinking and washing, fish for food, and a safe environment where they can raise their goats and hens. Their relationship with the river, as that of Hindus toward the holy Ganges, is one of submission and faith, and is not dictated by a desire to dominate or exploit it. Sita loves her home, especially the ancient peepal tree that "symbolize[s] the harmony between man and nature" (Bond, "Gentle Shade" 35), because it had stood firm when a great flood ravaged the area over twenty years before, and the island was completely submerged under water. It is a safe, carefree world, where Sita roams freely. Although the river shelters them from the intrusions of the outside world, it also offers a means of communication with the nearby villages and district town.

Sita does not go to school or get any formal education, but she is not ignorant. Her education is provided by her grandparents, with whom she has a loving relationship. Her grandmother has taught her all the things a girl must learn—cooking, cleaning, keeping house, and nurturing the sick—and from her grandfather she has learned most of the things that boys must know, like fishing and maneuvering the boat on the river. She knows the stories from Hindu mythology of Krishna, Indra, and Hanuman; the legend of the sacred peepal tree; and stories of good and bad spirits. Her only playmate is a ragdoll, Mumta, which she has made with the help of her grandmother and to whom she confides her innermost thoughts and secrets.

Bond does not dwell on the harsher aspects of his characters' lives: the poverty, the difficulties faced by the old couple, Sita's loneliness at her mother's untimely death and separation from her father who works in a factory a hundred miles away, and Sita's lack of companionship with children her own age. The "charm" of the characters rests in the rustic simplicity of their lives. Sita and her grandparents live in harmony with nature, reflecting a spiritual attitude that is free from the mundane and acquisitive values of urban life. While the setting and characters typify a pastoral idyll, the action of *Angry River* focuses on the protagonist's dynamic confrontation with nature. As the novel opens, Sita's comfortable relationship with the river, or nature, is about to undergo a profound change. With the onset of the monsoon rains—which are ordinarily most welcome after the stifling summer heat—the usually benign river transforms before Sita's very eyes.

> The sound of the river had always been with them, although they were seldom aware of it; but that night they noticed a change in its sound. There was something like a moan, like a wind in the tops of tall trees, and a swift hiss as the water swept round the rocks and carried away pebbles. And sometimes there was a rumble, as loose earth fell into the water. (19–20)

With the river fierce and angry, and with the thunder booming down from the hills, Sita is left alone on the island when Grandfather takes his ailing wife to the hospital in the nearby district town of Shahganj. As the river rises to flood levels and erodes the soil around the island, she saves their few precious belongings in an old tin trunk. Worried about her own safety and the welfare of her grandparents, she prays to Indra, god of thunder, and to all the other gods her grandmother has taught her about, but they do not appear to listen to her pleas. Sita confides her worst fears in her doll, Mumta, that perhaps the gods who are up in the mountains are angry with her. Mumta—who seems to be Sita's inner voice—questions Sita on why the natural disaster is directed at her personally. The gods, Sita responds, "don't have to have a reason for being angry. They are angry with everything, and we are in the middle of everything" (29).

The narrative incorporates several such postmodern devices that enable Sita to view her behavior and attitudes from the outside; she evaluates her experiences as she is undergoing them. At this crucial moment in her life, when she is absolutely alone and threatened with danger, Sita tries to make sense of her shattered physical world and her place in the cosmic order. It is through her ragdoll, Mumta, who although made up of bits and pieces of materials is symbolic of wholeness amidst chaos and disarray, that Sita achieves the objective distancing necessary to reflect on her relationship with the infinite powers. She does not passively accept the simple explanation that she is being punished for some transgression—her karma from this life or some previous lives. Rather, she engages in dialectical reasoning. Sita tries to review her relationship with nature and with the gods by analyzing her own relationship with her doll. Since she would save Mumta—who is her creation, just as she is the gods'—from the flood and would not abandon her, she wonders if the gods are even aware of her existence. Sita tries to understand the phenomena of rain and flood from her knowledge of Hindu mythology. From her grandmother, she has probably heard about Brahman, the omnipotent and omnipresent Supreme Being, in Its three aspects or functions as Creator (Brahma), Preserver (Vishnu), and Destroyer (Shiva). She now develops an impersonal image of the river as the Destroyer; it is unrecognizable to her in its present transformation into "a wild beast, a dragon on the rampage, thundering down from the hills and sweeping across the plain, bringing with it dead animals, uprooted trees, household goods, and huge fish choked to death by the swirling mud" (48–49).

Once the water begins to enter the hut, Sita is panic-stricken, and hastily climbs to the safety of the peepal. She sees that "the world has become one vast river" (33), as an assortment of objects from their hut and other huts float by her in utter confusion—bloated cattle, a kerosene can with hens perched on it, Grandfather's turban, a cane chair, cigarettes, wooden slippers, and a plastic doll. As Mumta, whom she had left behind in the hut in her haste and carelessness, also floats past her, Sita comes to understand her own relationship with the gods and nature in a clearer light. In that one moment, hanging on as she is for dear life to the branches of the ancient tree, she wonders how the gods who have created the whole universe can notice her alone, when she forgot her own doll. Overcome by the "power and size of the river," she experiences a "sense of smallness in a vast world, and a sense of place which is not merely geographical but also emotional" (Review of *Angry River* 804).

As Sita is perched on the tree, even this security is taken away from her. The peepal is no longer young; it groans and creaks as the river washes away the soil from its roots, and eventually floats down the river with Sita gripping its branches. Because of its great size, the tree moves slowly and lodges in a sandbank at a bend in the river. Sita's situation is paralleled with the fate of a mother crow who has a nest in the tree. From the branches of the tree, Sita observes the crow's nest being overturned and the eggs falling one by one into the river. The crow flies overhead, hoping that something has remained in the tree, but in the end she has to accept the inevitable. Once again, Bond introduces an episode that forces Sita to externalize her situation. Like the crow, Sita is reconciled to her loss of Mumta and her changed relationship with nature. With this detached attitude, Sita feels no guilt that she is being punished for her sins and realizes that the angry river is not an instrument of the gods' wrath but a manifestation of the duality of nature.

Despite the destruction and the hopelessness, Bond does not present a mournful view of life. Sita sees people in the distance escaping with their belongings from flooded villages in flat-bottomed boats. One boatload of villagers even points to her in an attempt to rescue her, but the surging river just shoves the boat away. A young boy named Krishan mysteriously appears in a boat from the foothills, seeking help for his flooded village, and the river sweeps him toward Sita. "We cannot fight the river," he tells Sita, "we must go wherever it takes us" (59). Krishan rows Sita to the relative safety of the flooded forest, tethers the boat to a tree, and gives her mangoes to satisfy her hunger. Like the animals of the forest who can be seen fleeing from their flooded lairs looking for shelter, Sita and Krishan are united in their common terror of the flood and their need to reach safety.

Embedded in the linear narrative are episodes and "invisible cultural codes," to use Steven Cohan and Linda Shires's term (115), that link Sita's experiences with those of mythological characters and prompt readers to view her fate with the same sense of awe and wonder associated with the stories of the gods. As any Hindu child who has been entertained with stories from the Sanskrit epics would have done, Sita wonders about the identity of Krishan. He reminds her of Lord Krishna, an incarnation of God Vishnu.[3] In Hindu mythology, Vishnu descends to earth from time to time in animal or human form to restore righteousness, to protect the innocent, and to help his devotees in distress. Lord Krishna's devotees lovingly refer to him as Krishan and Sham, the blue god.[4] In *Angry River*, when Krishan's dark skin, which looks blue in the moonlight, reminds Sita of Lord Krishna, she dismisses the thought from her mind by telling herself that he is just a village boy, although there is something different about him. Sita sleeps peacefully and dreams that Krishan and Krishna are one. In her dream, she flies with Lord Krishna on a great white bird—reminiscent of Vishnu's mount Garuda, a white eaglelike mythical bird—over the high Himalayas to the realm of the gods.[5] When Sita awakens to the sound of a baby elephant trumpeting for its mother, Krishan soothes her back to sleep with the music of his flute. The sweet sounds of the flute carry her back into her dream of riding with the Lord on the white bird.

This subconscious layer of dream sequences allows the reader to associate fictional time with mythic time and to place the story at a deeper allegorical level. Bond's choice of names firmly anchors the story in the Hindu tradition. That these names are significant and purposeful is obvious when one compares them to the names Bond chose for earlier versions of the story (Papers). Mumta—a Hindi word for the all-encompassing love that mothers feel for their children—was called by the Anglicized name of Miss Rita in the first draft of the novel, which would have been highly inappropriate because of Sita's rural background and lack of familiarity with the Westernized segment of the Indian population. Likewise, Krishan was originally named Bhim, a character in the *Mahabharat* known for his strength; and in the longer version of the story he is called Vijay, meaning victory. Sita is the name of the heroine of the Sanskrit epic *Ramayan*, whose hero Rama, like Krishna, is worshipped as an incarnation of God Vishnu. Hindus worship Sita as the Divine Mother because she was beautiful and gentle, and because she accepted suffering without a murmur (Das 28).

Sita's dream of flying on a white bird also reminds one of an episode from the *Ramayan* in which Garuda tries to save the heroine Sita from Ravana, the evil king of Lanka, but it is her husband, Rama, who invades the technologically superior kingdom of Lanka and rescues her. While Krishna and Sita come from two different sacred-epic texts, to Hindus, who worship them as personal gods, they represent the incarnations of God Vishnu and his consort Lakshmi, the bestower of material wealth and domestic happiness. Thus, these intertextual references and codes manipulate the reader's perspective to regard the principal characters of *Angry River*, Sita and Krishan, as the divine couple who are reincarnated again and again on earth to help alleviate human suffering.

In addition to Bond's use of traditional Hindu names, he links the central episode of the novel with the Hindu myths of the great deluge. When Krishan saves Sita from the flood, the reader is reminded of the childhood deeds of Lord Krishna, who rescued the village of Gokul when heavy rains and flooding threatened to destroy it. Krishna lifted Mount Goverdhan with his little finger so that both cattle and villagers could take refuge beneath it. Peace with nature and themselves returned to the villagers of Gokul because Krishna cared deeply for them and "every living thing seemed to bloom and blossom with awareness of his presence" (*Krishnaleela*, no pag.). Krishan's mysterious appearance in a boat to rescue Sita is reminiscent of an even earlier myth of the flood, when King Satyavrat, who was doing penance on the bank of a river, was warned of a heavy rainfall that would result in the destruction of the world. Satyavrat was told that a boat and a fish to whom he had been kind (none other than God Vishnu), would appear mysteriously, and that he would be taken to a new world where, known as Manu, he would be the founder of the human race.

Further parallels can be drawn from Bond's diary entries, which reveal the author's strong emotional response to Lord Krishna and the flood theme. For instance, while traveling in northern India, he writes on August 14, 1960: "At Mathura [the birthplace of Lord Krishna], it rained as heavily as it must have done the day Krishna was born. Sheets of rain. In a few seconds, people were drenched to the skin, and within ten minutes the roads were completely flooded. Oddly enough, it was Krishna's birthday" (Papers). According to the *Bhagavatam*, Krishna's birth was heralded by heavy monsoon rains that enabled his father, Vasudev, to take the newborn infant to the village of Gokul across the Jamuna River in order to escape certain death at the hands of the wicked ruler Kans.

Finally, Bond also incorporates the symbolic meaning of Lord Krishna's flute into the story. To Hindus, Krishna's flute-playing is the sensual equivalent of the quickening of life, the transcendental unifying spirit of god and nature; one's joy in His music is considered a symbolic submission to the divine will. Sita's fascination with Krishan's flute is reminiscent of Lord Krishna's childhood, when the "maidens of the forest [on] hearing his flute would rush to him, losing as it were their sense of separate being" (*Krishnaleela*, no pag.). Like Lord Krishna, who was raised as a cowherd by foster parents, Krishan of *Angry River* is also the son of a humble cowherd, and he too plays the flute to express his harmony with creation. When Krishan parts from Sita once the rain stops, he gives his flute to her as a token of his promise to return, just as the divine Krishna had promised Radha, his favorite and most devoted village maiden, that he would return to her. Krishan's giving the flute to Sita, and offering to teach her how to play it, also symbolizes regeneration: the coming together of the male-female forces, of Purusha (pure consciousness) and Prakriti (nature).

With the help of a kind farmer, Sita finds her grandfather in Shahganj, but Grandmother is dead. Just as she had accepted the destructive form of the river earlier, Sita now accepts her grandmother's death as a natural phase in the wheel of life, and realizes that her old grandfather will now have to rely on her. When the water recedes, they sadly return to the island, and the cycle of life is renewed. Together, Sita and Grandfather rebuild their lives; they build another hut against the big rock, plant a mango tree between the two protective rocks where the peepal had once flourished, and fish for food. In exchange for the doll that she has lost, a brightly colored wooden peacock is swept ashore on the island, almost like a reincarnation of Mumta. Something from the past—Grandfather's ancient hookah that she had stowed away in the trunk—is also saved as they begin their new lives. The river is once again life-sustaining.

The story of Sita comes full circle with the resumption of a peaceful, normal life on the island and in the many villages along the banks of the river, but the story of her spiritual quest has just begun. Sita thinks often of Krishan and his flute and lives with the hope of seeing him again. Although Sita is unable to play the flute, she thinks it plays by itself, as she can hear its mysterious and entrancing sounds wafting through the air. When she has given up all hope, Krishan returns. The two children sit on the river's edge and dangle their feet in the cool blue water. Sita, remembering the fearful experiences they had shared, remarks on the dual aspects of the river, "Sometimes the river is angry, and sometimes it is kind" (87). Krishan, in response, urges Sita to perceive the river as a whole and to try to fathom its mystical nature. "We are a part of the river," he tells her. "We cannot live without it" (87).

With Krishan's simple remark, Bond touches on the debate between the dualistic and nondualistic schools of philosophy. Dualism contends that in striving for the truth, the mind has to divide things into parts before understanding the whole, while nondualism propounds that the mind, limited by its reasoning ability, leads people to half truths and fear, because it perceives the external appearance rather than the reality within. According to the Advaita school of nondualism and the Upanishads, which form the basis of Vedanta philosophy, the mind, or thought, is the creator of duality. It places everything in a subject-object relationship; hence, the mind is fragmented and can perceive, for example, light only in relation to darkness, death in relation to birth, and creation in relation to destruction.[6]

Krishan's gentle remark is intended to direct Sita beyond her dichotomous thinking to the higher level of understanding the multifaceted and simultaneous attributes of the river. Krishan's words are reminiscent of Lord Krishna's discourse in the *Mahabharat*, which forms the subject matter of the *Bhagavad Gita*, where He reveals his mystic form to the Pandava hero, Arjuna, to dispel his fear of death and the destruction of the self. In Lord Krishna, Arjuna sees "The whole world there united" (Edgerton 13) and exclaims in awe and wonder:

> No end nor middle nor yet beginning of Thee
> Do I see, O All-God, All-Formed! (Edgerton 16)

Like Lord Krishna, Krishan tries to help Sita relate to the river as to the macrocosm, or the totality of everything in the universe. Perhaps, like Arjuna, Sita will learn that nothing is destroyed, and that everything, all objects, dead or living, exist in the river. In progressing from an active intellectual state to calm philosophical contemplation in her communion with nature, Sita is one step closer to a disciplined search or awareness of the enlightened state of *moksha*, or nirvana.

In the final paragraphs of the novel, Bond leads the reader away from emotional involvement in Sita's experiences to reflection on the meaning of her relationship with the river.

> It was a good river, deep and strong, beginning in the mountains and ending in the sea.

> Along its banks, for hundreds of miles, lived millions of people, and Sita was only one small girl among them, and no one had ever heard of her, no one knew her—except for the old man, and the boy, and the river. (87–88)

The ending allows the reader to contemplate the transient nature of everything that is created. The outward illusory world of *maya*, which is rooted in time, place, and causality, will perish in due course and will be replaced, just as the peepal tree and the doll were, but the river will remain the same despite the changes it undergoes. As the river flows through the length and breadth of India, it mystically unifies all the diverse people who dwell on its shores even though they do not know each other: old and young, male and female, sick and healthy, rich and poor, animal and plants, city dwellers and villagers, gods and devotees, and past, present, and future. The river is eternal, a divine manifestation that has all the attributes of the all-encompassing Brahman, and Sita is a part of this totality. The changing moods of the river symbolize the cosmic dance of the universe, a continuous process of creation, preservation, and reabsorption.

If one wonders how a poor and uneducated village girl such as Sita can be expected to engage in such sophisticated philosophical reasoning, one need only be reminded that Sita has communed with nature all her life, and has the capacity to understand the divine rhythm behind the duality of nature. Bond has the highest regard for children and for the unlettered villagers. He once said that "children are as intelligent as adults, they only have less experience" (qtd. in Chatterjee 7). Bond states that when he wrote *Angry River*, his close association with and participation in the lives of the simple hill folk of the Himalayas led to his naturally absorbing Hindu mythology and culture as a living experience (Interview).

HARMONY WITH THE RHYTHMS OF NATURE

Other stories that focus on the destructive aspects of nature are *Flames in the Forest* (recently reprinted as "Riding through the Flames") and *Earthquake*. In the former, eleven-year-old Romi is caught in a forest fire as he is returning home from school. However, he braves the burning forest to deliver medicine to his father for his backache. The tension and excitement of the story are well handled as Romi and the animals flee in terror through the enveloping flames to the safety of the river. Romi's calm and confident demeanor that he will reach the river in time is contrasted with the panic of young Teju, whom he helps. If in *Angry River* the river is a destructive force, in *Flames in the Forest* it becomes a symbol of hope and survival as Romi, Teju, and the animals flee to it from the burning forest. As assorted animals and the boys unite in its safety, the river becomes a symbol of the essential harmony of all creation. The elephants, python, and jackal do not harm the boys because they are all trying to escape from their common enemy: fire. Bond focuses on yet another natural disaster in *Earthquake*. According to the author, it was written for Mukesh (Prem Singh's younger son), "who liked upheavals" ("Writer" 3). The plot does not focus on the experiences of one major character but gives the simultaneous experiences of the various members of the Burman household during an earthquake in Shillong, Assam, an area prone to earthquakes. Every brick and masonry building in town crumbles, whereas the wooden structures of the poor survive by swaying with the tremors of the earth. The earthquake wipes away all social distinctions between the rich and poor, high caste and low caste, as the Burmans are forced to seek refuge in their servant's humble home. Although material possessions are lost, what really matters endures: mutual respect, family unity, and love for fellow human beings. Grandfather Burman's bathing ritual through good and bad times symbolizes his philosophic acceptance of the vagaries of life—happiness and sorrow, good luck and misfortune. Like Sita and her grandfather in *Angry River*, the Burmans decide not to flee Shillong because no place is free of natural disasters, indicating the characters' acceptance of the duality of nature. This story is reminiscent of "Grandfather's Earthquake," an essay that provides factual information on the earthquake that ravaged the states of Bengal and Assam on June 12, 1897. In addition to this journalistic research, Bond introduces a fictional element into the essay by placing his Grandfather Bond in the midst of the disaster in order to individualize the experiences of the Anglo-Indian community of Shillong.

Through these stories of flood, fire, and earthquake, Bond illustrates that personal happiness should not be dependent solely on material pleasures, because they are transitory. However, he does not advocate self-denial or nonparticipation in the routine activities of daily existence; he only suggests that an acceptance of the fierce and benign aspects of nature will lead to harmony with creation. This view of nature is perfectly in accord with the Hindu concept of the duality of the gods, who are perceived in both their benevolent and fierce, or *ghora*, manifestations. Bond's vision, and consequently that of his fictional characters, is a natural outcome of living close to nature.

ANIMALS SHOULD HAVE RIGHTS ON EARTH

Bond's earlier animal stories—such as those in *Grandfather's Private Zoo*—were idealized and whimsical stories meant to amuse young readers by showing the respect and care that the protagonists have for animals. However, the later stories portray the natural aggression in the battle for food and survival between predator and victim—between frog and heron, mongoose and cobra, eagle and hare. It is the law of the jungle that animals feed off each other. "Sudden death appears at intervals. Wild creatures do not have to think about it, and so the sudden killing of one of their number by some predator of the forest is only a fleeting incident soon forgotten by the survivors" ("Tiger, Tiger" 107).

As with nature, there is dualism in the relationship between animals and humans. In stories where animals are the adversaries of humans, either animals are struggling to survive, hunters have wounded the predator, or humans have upset the ecological balance by encroaching into the animal's domain. These three types of stories provide a thought-provoking treatment of the plight of wild animals in India. Bond's plea is that predatory animals are part of the duality of nature; hence, we need to protect them, allow them their space on earth.

Panther's Moon and Other Stories, a collection of ten animal stories, mostly set in remote Himalayan villages where predatory animals can still be found, explores these various relationships between humans and animals. Life is hard for the hill folk as they face the constant threat of wild animals; moreover, medical help is usually far away in a neighboring town, and they have to rely on each other. Bond's simple yet elegant prose matches the lifestyle of the characters and the ordinary events of their lives, but the language and events become charged with dramatic intensity when a man-eater enters the village. In "The Tiger in the Tunnel," a battle for survival is fought between a tiger and the night watchman, whose duty is to make sure that the tunnel is free of obstruction before the mail train passes through. One night, a man-eater walks straight at him from the tunnel, and the two adversaries are locked in deadly combat, each fighting for his life. Although the watchman wounds the tiger with his razor-sharp ax, he is easily killed by the tiger. But the tiger, with the ax lodged in his shoulder, is unable to move out of the path of the approaching train and is cut in half. However, life must go on, and the battle for survival is now passed to the next generation. Tembu, the watchman's son, after performing the last rites, assumes his father's job in order to help feed the family.

A different type of predator is encountered in "The Eye of the Eagle."[7] The protagonist, Jai, studies in a school in the village of Maku, where his parents grow rice on terraced fields and his grandparents graze their herd of lambs. Grandfather encourages Jai to study, but he also has to do chores at home—chopping wood, grazing the herd, planting rice, and hoeing and tilling. The relationship between Jai and his grandparents is loving and nurturing, as their wisdom is passed down to the younger generation. Jai helps his grandparents by spending the October holidays with them in the upper elevations of the Tung range, at 12,000 feet above sea level, where there is sweet green grass. This Himalayan region is beautifully described in the essay "The Magic of Tungnath": "The brushwood Rhododendrons are the last trees on our ascent, for as we approach Tungnath, the treeline ends and there is nothing between earth and sky except grass and rock and tiny flowers" (45).

In Tung, danger is ever present in the form of a golden eagle—the "king of the skies over the higher Himalayas" (74)—which preys on the small animals with its powerful beak, talons, and wings that spread to eight feet. One day, while Jai and his shaggy guard dog, Motu, are grazing the herd, the golden eagle picks up a small lamb and takes it to its eyrie on a cliff above Tung. The eagle is a difficult adversary; while Motu can keep leopards and wolves away, he is not so successful with the clever eagle. Jai realizes that in order to protect the herd he will have to be more careful. However, the eagle is not seen as evil, because it will prey on anything that comes in its territory. Jai even admires its intelligence, its ability to think critically, and to plan an attack based on Jai's moves. The terms "graceful" and "majestic" are employed to depict the eagle's courage in going after the herd.

When Motu is wounded after heroically saving a lamb, he has to stay at home to recuperate, and now it is a battle between the eagle and the boy. When Jai beats off the bird with his grandfather's stick, a substitute for Motu, the brave eagle is not afraid. "Instead it landed on the hillside and glared at the boy, as a king would glare at a humble subject who had dared to pelt him with a pebble" (81). At the climactic moment, the wounded bird fearlessly continues to attack Jai as he tries to save a lamb. Jai and the lamb tumble into the protection of a thorny bilberry bush, and Jai loses his stick. Another eagle, perhaps the mate to the first one, comes to attack the herd, and Jai shouts for help, because animals of prey can be scared off by groups of humans. Motu comes barking from the house, and Grandma bangs two pots to scare the predatory birds. The frightened eagles leave, but the family decides to move down to Maku the next day because it has started to snow.

"Very soon the bears and the leopards and the golden eagles would have the high ranges all to themselves" (79).

The second type of story involves a person from the outside world, usually a *shikari* ("hunter") who has wounded a tiger or panther without killing it, hence forcing the animal to become a man-eater. Set in the village of Manjari in the Garhwal District, *Panther's Moon*[8] is the story of twelve-year-old Bisnu's encounter with a predator that has taken many victims. When Bisnu learns that a panther has been on the prowl in the neighboring village, he has to be cautious while making the daily five-mile trek to school, and the villagers also stop going alone through the forest after dark. However, death comes to Manjari when Bisnu's pet dog, Sheroo, who always accompanies Bisnu to school, is killed by the panther. Readers are aware that had the panther not eaten Sheroo, it would surely have been Bisnu who died. Tension builds once the panther starts stalking the village at night, even dragging victims from their homes. It is a fact that a man-eating panther, unlike a tiger, does not lose its fear of humans, and hence will try to secure its victim at night and even attempt to break into their houses (see Corbett xvi).

While returning from school one day, Bisnu saves the life of a lone kid. He hears the rasping of the panther and, taking the kid under his arm, climbs up a spruce tree, because its branches are not strong enough to take the weight of a panther. Bond carefully describes the well-orchestrated battle of wits that follows, and the thought processes of Bisnu and the panther as they face each other in the night. The panther tries to distract Bisnu and catch him off guard:

> Bisnu remained motionless in the tree...but the kid began bleating. The panther looked up, and gave its deepthroated, rasping grunt—a fearsome sound, calculated to strike terror into any tree-borne animal. Many a monkey, petrified by a panther's roar, has fallen from its perch to make a meal for Mr. Spots. The man-eater was trying the same technique on Bisnu. (44)

Bisnu remembers his father's words that one should look a panther in the eye and not let him know that you are afraid. He is saved from this particular encounter only when he begins to shout, and his neighbors organize a search party to look for him. The panther leaves for another village, where he kills several people.

This elemental battle between the villagers and the panther continues when the man-eater returns to Manjari. Bisnu, who has stopped going to school because of the danger, feels that the panther is his personal adversary because he is faced with the possibility of failing his exams and of not being able to get a good job to support his mother and sister, Puja. One night, the panther scratches at Bisnu's door, trying to pry it open, but Bisnu manages to crawl up the skylight and surprise the panther by spearing its back. The panther retreats in pain, but returns another day when Bisnu and Puja are working in the terraced fields. Bisnu warns Puja as the panther is about to pounce on her, and when she jumps out of the way, the animal loses its footing and falls in a pit. With the help of Bisnu, the villagers kill the man-eater. With the danger over—till the next man-eater comes—Bisnu returns to school and does well on his exams.

Throughout this battle for survival, readers come to admire both Bisnu's and the panther's courage. The panther has no other way of feeding himself because of a bullet he received in his leg the previous year. He has to depend on capturing domestic animals from the isolated villages, or on killing humans. In the Himalayas, the presence of tigers and panthers is accepted as a part of life. They remain in the forests, hunting deer and other wild animals, and rarely come near human dwellings unless an imbalance is created by a careless hunter who wounds the animal but does not finish the job. When I questioned the author about the happy ending—at least for the protagonist—he replied: "Well, children's publishers are disinclined to publish stories with unhappy endings! I had to reduce the man-eater's victims to satisfy the editors at Random House" (Telephone conversation).

Bond's dismay at human encroachment into the territory of the predator, and the losing battle that the animal is fighting in present-day India, is expressed in "The Leopard." In this story, a leopard comes to trust a nature-loving human, who enjoys visiting a forest near Mussoorie. The protagonist says that he has not come to take anything from the forest, only "to renew myself, both physically and mentally" (62). All the birds and animals—including the leopard—cast off their "protective fear" (67) and accept him as part of the forest. The protagonist becomes uneasy when illegal trophy hunters from the city learn of the leopard's presence and want to shoot it for its skin. On one of his walks through the forest, he sees the leopard being carried on a pole by the hunters, and he blames himself: "Perhaps I had made him confident—too confident, too careless, too trusting of the human in his midst" (67). As he walks back sadly, the forest "was very silent, almost as though the birds and animals knew that their trust had been violated" (67). Bond sincerely believes that we have been entrusted to preserve and protect our environment and wildlife, a trust that has been broken because of human greed and carelessness.

"Tiger, Tiger Burning Bright" is a more hopeful story about the future of wildlife. It is about a majestic old tiger who had lived peacefully near a village in the foothills of the Himalayas, with the villagers and tiger respecting each other's territory.[9] By focalizing the viewpoint of the tiger, readers learn how the clever old tiger had managed to evade trophy hunters. However, when the tall grasses are dry as a result of a delay in the monsoon rains, some careless refugee settlers start a forest fire, and the tiger's natural habitat is destroyed overnight. He stays hungry for days until he is forced to attack the villagers' buffaloes. Because it is a question of either the tiger's survival or theirs, the villagers organize a hunt. They ambush the tiger on the bridge and shoot him. Luckily, the slightly wounded tiger falls in the Ganges and is carried to the opposite bank, where he finds a favorable habitat and a mate. The villagers miss the tiger, because he signified dignity and the harmony of creation and, more practically, he had provided protection from intruders who have now started cutting the trees, which will eventually lead to soil erosion, flooding, and the destruction of their lives. The tiger is considered the very "soul" of India, and the story is a strong plea for the preservation of wildlife. It illustrates that tigers and panthers turn into man-eaters only because of human greed and fear, rapid deforestation, and upsetting of the jungle ecology.

These stories of man-eaters, in particular, remind one of the many real-life adventures of Major Jim Corbett, who served in the British Army in India and was called upon numerous times to dispatch man-eaters in the Kumaon hills, one of whom had killed 434 people before Corbett heard about it.[10] To the villagers, Corbett was a savior, and there is a permanent memorial to him near Rudraprayag, which Bond has visited. Bond agrees with Corbett that a tiger is not "deliberately cruel" or "bloodthirsty" and unless provoked, it does not kill more than it needs "to satisfy its hunger or the hunger of its cubs" (Corbett xviii). Although Corbett spent over three decades in regular pursuit of man-eaters, he concludes that "a tiger is a large-hearted gentleman with boundless courage and that when he is exterminated—as exterminated he will be unless public opinion rallies to his support—India will be the poorer by having lost the finest of her fauna" (xviii).

To hunters, the jungle is the ultimate test of manhood—physical endurance, overcoming fears, outsmarting the animal, and control over nature—but to Bond, it teaches respect for wildlife and the environment. He is against exploiting wild animals for entertainment (circus), sport and trophies (hunting), or money (selling skins). In his *shikar* stories, such as "A Week in the Jungle," Bond uses words like "slaughtering" and "bloodthirsty" to describe the hunters as sportsmen. While he is antihunting, he believes that we can kill animals for food "because even animals killed for food; but not for pleasure" ("A Week" 71).

Even in the cities, where there are no predatory animals, Bond regrets that some humans lack generosity in their behavior toward animals. He has written several stories in which an animal becomes an instrument of punishment and justice for humans who deserve it. For example, in "A Crow for All Seasons," a satirical story about human unconcern for birds and beasts, the events are seen from the perspective of a house crow, Speedy, who scavenges from a bungalow inhabited by the Colonel, his memsahib, their son, and Junior sahib, a good-for-nothing nephew who lives with them. Speedy thinks that Junior sahib is worse than the crows because he does not work for a living but free-loads off his relatives. While the Colonel and his wife give Speedy scraps of food or do not object to his eating from the garbage cans, Junior sahib is vicious and throws things at him. When Junior sahib shoots Speedy's cousin, all good-natured fun is over, and the entire crow community begins to peck and claw him every time he ventures out of the house ("'Elephants never forget, and crows never forgive,' says the Colonel" [95]). Junior sahib has a nervous breakdown, and the family takes him to the hills to recover. When Speedy appears on the verandah of the resthouse, Junior sahib completely loses his mind and imagines himself to be a crow; he is having "[d]elusions of grandeur," says the memsahib (99). The story ends happily when the family returns home and Junior sahib starts to feed the crows every day. "A Crow for All Seasons" is an unveiled attack on the selfish and unpredictable behavior of humans toward animals.

While Bond is opposed to the destruction of wildlife, he is not sentimental. Wild animals belong in their natural habitat and not in his house, he says. The poems in *Granny's Tree Climbing* pray that there should be room for everyone in this world, even for elephants, who "do take up space" ("Room for Elephants" [26]), and "May the tiger's roar be heard" but that tigers should not be so numerous that one "Might be tempted to come into my bedroom / In search of a meal!" ("Tigers Forever" [27]).

A TIGER NEEDS A JUNGLE

As an environmentalist, Bond is concerned about human encroachment into the forests in the Himalayan region, hence disturbing the balance between the animal and human worlds. While he does not intend his stories to call for political or social action, his child heroes do not live in a vacuum. Their experiences raise one's consciousness to the necessity of protecting our environment, because the leopard and tiger are nearing extinction in India as a result of rapid deforestation. With a human population of over 1 billion, more space is needed for housing, farming, grazing livestock, and factories. But this human expansion, he believes, has taken place "at the expense of other creatures and the forest and plant life that has sustained us. God may be forgiving, but Nature is not, and we upset the ecological balance at our own peril" ("Rani" 5). His stories "remind the younger generation, the inheritors of the earth, of the denuding process of the beautiful planet earth" (Menon 65–66). They make the sensitive reader understand the serious consequences of cutting trees and destroying nature for short-term material gain.

Like the ancient Hindu *rishis*, Bond believes that trees are sacred. He writes, "shade-giving trees symbolise the harmony between man and nature, and that our ancestors, in their devotion to trees, and reverence for them, clearly showed that they knew what was good for them" ("Gentle Shade" 35). Bond pleads that trees are important to the birds and animals who live in the forests, as well as to humans for fruit and timber, for attracting rain, and for preventing soil erosion and keeping the desert away (*Once upon a Monsoon* 55). He also believes that trees have a spiritually uplifting influence on humans. In describing the forests of the Himalayas in "The Magic of Tungnath," he writes: "one comes away a better man, forest-refreshed, and more aware of what the earth was really like before mankind began to strip it bare" (43).

Bond's children's book *Dust on the Mountain* is a fictional account of the environmental destruction that has taken place on the hills near Mussoorie. It is a combination of two stories—"The Summer Season" and "The Last Truck Ride"—that were published earlier in *Time Stops at Shamli and Other Stories.* After an unusual winter without rain or snow and an equally dry summer without the monsoons, Bisnu, the hill boy who first appeared in *Panther's Moon*, decides to go down to Mussoorie to find work in order to provide for his mother and sister. The ground is hard and unsuitable for cultivation, the trees are without leaves or fruit, and a forest fire caused by the carelessness of a woodcutter is raging on the next mountain. The villagers have learned to be patient, but Bisnu is a courageous boy who wants to shape his own destiny. On his way to Mussoorie by bus, he is surprised to find that there are no trees on the hills, a sight that would be unthinkable in his village. An elderly passenger, who is going to Mussoorie for medical treatment because no doctor will come to his village, tells him that "[r]ich men from the cities come here and buy up what they want—land, houses, trees, people!" (14). He warns Bisnu not to get tempted by the lure of big cities: "It is better to be hungry in your village than to be hungry on the streets of Bombay" (15).

Bisnu easily finds a job at the tea shop of the Picture Palace movie theater, where he works with two other boys and sleeps in the foyer of the cinema hall at night. Bisnu is amazed at the tourists, and at the expensively dressed city women with make-up, but he is also homesick: "The hill-station, with all its glitter, was just a pretty gift box with nothing inside; a body without a soul" (24).

At the end of September, when the season is over, the movie theater closes for the winter. Bisnu and his co-worker, Chittru, decide to work in a limestone quarry further down the mountains. As they near the quarries, an eight-mile walk downhill from Mussoorie, there is choking dust everywhere. The hills are bare and dry, and there is no vegetation or animals, except a lizard, in this desertlike place. Bisnu recalls the variety of trees in his village and wonders if the same thing will happen there someday. He is shocked by the devastation caused by the blasting: "There was a sharp crack of explosives and the hillside blossomed outwards. Earth and rocks hurtled down the mountain" and "shrubs and small trees were flung into the air" (36). He gets a job helping a truck driver who transports the stones to the depot at the bottom of the mountain. Pritam Singh is good-natured, but in order to make two trips a day he speeds down the hairpin bends of the narrow mountain road. One day, when he is in a particularly buoyant mood and is driving dangerously close to the edge of the road, a mule comes into his path. As he swerves to avoid it, the truck plunges over the side of the mountain. Luckily, an old oak tree stops the truck from hurtling down to the bottom of the mountain. Although badly hurt, Pritam Singh knows that he owes his life to the lone tree. He decides to retire and live with his well-off son, while Bisnu returns to Manjari to farm: "It's better to grow things on the land than to blast things out of it" (44–45). As a good omen, it snows heavily and Bisnu returns to his village full of hope for the future. This story not only presents the harsh reality of Bisnu's life, but there is a sense of sadness in the realization that the changes appearing in the Himalayan villages are due to contact with the urban world, which the author sees as aggressive and acquisitive.

While Bond understands that humans need trees to feed their livestock and to build their homes, what he cannot understand is why they cannot replace what they have taken from nature. "If people keep cutting trees, instead of planting them, there'll soon be no forests left at all, and the world will be just one vast desert" ("My Father's Trees" 145). There is a wonderful ceremony in India called Vanamoho-utsav, when all over the country people plant trees. Bond's hometown has given new meaning to this annual festival by replanting entire hillsides in Mussoorie. This ongoing reforestation project—called the ECO Task Force—was established for this purpose in the early 1980s by the Indian Army stationed in Landour Cantonment. The Task Force "adopts" certain hillsides, and then plants and maintains the new trees. Bond has supported the project by accepting invitations to inaugurate the "planting" ceremonies. Another project, started in the 1970s, is the more political and visible Chipko ("Hug the Tree") Movement, whose members offer nonviolent resistance to the cutting of trees.[11]

The theme of tree planting recurs in several of Bond's essays and stories. In the autobiographical *Once upon a Monsoon Time*, the protagonist and his father plant trees on a rocky island in a dry riverbed, hoping that the saplings will be left alone and that floods will not wash them away. "Just think—just imagine!—ten years from now this little island may be a green paradise, and birds and squirrels and insects will be living in the trees we've planted" (53). There is a sentimental description of the narrator's father holding out his arm to an old keekar tree, and "the crooked keekar, with its twisting, struggling branches, seemed to be reaching out to my father—reaching out like a cripple who wants to get up and walk" (56). In "My Father's Trees in Dehra," the protagonist, now an adult, revisits this spot and is amazed that the trees are thriving and that his father's dream has been realized.[12]

Like the protagonists of his nature stories, Bond has developed a loving relationship with trees. From the window seat in his bedroom, he can see the deodars, oaks, and maples on the hillside below: "The trees stand watch over my day-to-day life. They are the guardians of my conscience. I have no one else to answer to, so I live and work under the generous but highly principled supervision of the trees" (*Rain* 3). As a writer, he believes that the trees are his "best critics," because "[a]s long as I am aware of their presence, I can try to avoid the trivial and the banal" (*Rain* 3).

Nature images that occur frequently in Bond's writings are of a mountain pool, banyan tree, cherry tree, or an island of trees that have become small ecosystems representing the universe in a microcosm. A variety of insects, birds, and animals—and humans—come to these places to find a safe haven. All are equal in the presence of nature. Bond's belief in mystical unity, that we are all a tiny part of the great scheme of the Creator, is best embodied in *To Live in Magic*, where Nature serves as "the great unifier": "The gentleness of the author's vision takes us beyond the sophisticated ritual and pageantry of modern religions to a simpler, fresher, clearer world where man, nature and god are one" (Note to Parents and Teachers). Bond does not follow any organized religion; he is a worshipper of nature—of mountains, trees, flowers, and simple people. His nature poems and stories gently prod readers toward reexamining their relationship with nature, toward introspection and self-knowledge, and toward establishing harmony between the spiritual and material spheres. They offer a mode of creative inquiry by which "microcosmic man can be brought into harmony with the macrocosmic universe through visualization of the divine pattern" (Mehra 50).

> This leaf so complete in itself,
> is only part of a tree.
> . . .
> And the sea, so complete in itself,
> rests like a raindrop
> in the hand of god. ("Raindrop," *Granny's Tree Climbing* 33)

NOTES

1. This section is a slightly shortened version of my article "The River Is Eternal: Nature Mysticism and Vedanta Philosophy in Ruskin Bond's *Angry River*," *The Lion and the Unicorn* 19.2 (Dec. 1995): 253–68. Reprinted by permission.

2. Originally written as "Sita and the River," the present version is more unified and focused on the theme because it eliminates several episodes that are not directly related to the protagonist's relationship with the river. However, the title *Angry River*, although engaging, emphasizes the fierce aspects of the river and not its totality.

3. Krishna is the hero of the epic poem *Bhagavatam*, in which the poet-sage Vyasa celebrates the deeds and the ten incarnations of Vishnu, the Preserver. Krishna also figures in a secondary, though equally vital, role in another Sanskrit epic, the *Mahabharat*.

4. Lord Krishna is also called Radhe-Sham (beloved of Radha; Krishna and Radha also represent divine lovers); Bansuriwallah (one with the flute); Krishan-Gopal; and Krishan-Kanhiya.

5. Each god has his or her own mount or vehicle that is an object of worship by devotees of the god.

6. In his commentary on the Upanishads, Swami Nikhilananda states that "Proper understanding of the philosophy of Non-dualistic Vedanta depends upon the recognition of the two standpoints from which Truth can be observed. The one is the standpoint of the Relative; the other, the standpoint of the Absolute"; however, "duality disappears when the absolute Truth is known, and all the activities and thoughts associated with duality drop away" (41). Nikhilananda suggests that this holistic vision, or knowledge of Brahman, can be achieved by developing *bodhi*, or deeper consciousness, by withdrawing the senses from outer objects and concentrating on becoming more aware of deeper phases of existences (28).

7. "The Eye of the Eagle" was published in 1987 as *The Eyes of the Eagle* by Julia MacRae in its Blackbird Series.

8. *Panther's Moon* was originally published by Random House in 1969. A slightly shortened and revised version appeared in 1979 as *Night of the Leopard*, prepared for Hamish Hamilton to fit their Antelope Series.

9. "Tiger, Tiger Burning Bright" was published as *Tigers Forever* by Julia MacRae in 1983.

10. See Jim Corbett's *Man-Eaters of Kumaon.*

11. See Deborah Lee Rose's *The People Who Hugged Trees: An Environmental Folktale.*

12. This tree-planting incident is not based on an actual event from the author's life.

WORKS CITED

Angry River. Review. *Times Literary Supplement* [New Delhi] 14 July 1972: 804.

Bond, Ruskin. *Angry River.* 1972. Rpt. New Delhi: Rupa, 1992.

___. "A Crow for All Seasons." Bond, *Panther's Moon and Other Stories* 84–100.

___. *Dust on the Mountain.* London: Julia MacRae, 1990.

___. *Earthquake.* London: Julia MacRae, 1984.

___. "The Eye of the Eagle." Bond, *Panther's Moon and Other Stories* 74–83.

___. *Flames in the Forest.* London: Julia MacRae, 1981.

___. *Ganga Descends.* Dehra Dun: English Book Depot, 1992.

___. "Gentle Shade by Day." *A Garland of Memories.* By Bond. New Delhi: Mukul Prakashan, 1982. 33–35.

___. "Grandfather's Earthquake." *Strange Men, Strange Places.* By Bond. New Delhi: Rupa, 1992. 81–84.

___. *Grandfather's Private Zoo.* Bombay: India Book House, 1967.

___. *Granny's Tree Climbing and Other Poems*. Gurgaon: Scholastic, 2000.

___. Interview with Meena Khorana. Mussoorie, August 1992.

___. *An Island of Trees: Nature Stories and Poems*. New Delhi: Ratna Sagar, 1992.

___. "The Leopard." Bond, *Panther's Moon and Other Stories* 60–67.

___. "The Magic of Tungnath." Bond, *Ganga Descends* 43–48.

___. "My Father's Trees in Dehra." *Night Train at Deoli and Other Stories*. By Bond. New Delhi: Penguin, 1988. 138–48.

___. Note to Parents and Teachers. Bond, *To Live in Magic*, inside front cover.

___. *Once upon a Monsoon Time*. Hyderabad: Orient Longman, 1974.

___. *Panther's Moon*. Bond, *Panther's Moon and Other Stories* 27–56.

___. *Panther's Moon and Other Stories*. New Delhi: Puffin, 1991.

___. Papers. Mugar Memorial Library. Boston University, Boston.

___. *Rain in the Mountains: Notes from the Himalayas*. New Delhi: Viking/Penguin, 1993.

___. "Rani of the Doon." Bond, *Ganga Descends* 5–7.

___. "Sita and the River." *Collected Fiction*. By Bond. New Delhi: Penguin, 1999. 153–86.

___. Telephone conversation with Meena Khorana. 24 November 2001.

___. "The Tiger in the Tunnel." Bond, *Panther's Moon and Other Stories* 11–16.

___. "Tiger, Tiger Burning Bright." Bond, *Panther's Moon and Other Stories* 101–28.

___. *Time Stops at Shamli and Other Stories*. New Delhi: Penguin, 1989.

___. *To Live in Magic: A Book of Nature Poems*. New Delhi: Thomson, 1985.

___. "A Week in the Jungle." *Grandfather's Private Zoo*. By Bond. Bombay: India Book House, 1967. 71–80.

___. "Writer on the Hill." Bond, *Ganga Descends* 1–4.

Chatterjee, Manini. "The Other Bond." *Telegraph* [Calcutta] 8 Dec. 1991: 4–8.

Cohan, Steven, and Linda M. Shires. *Telling Stories: A Theoretical Analysis of Narrative Fiction*. New York and London: Routledge, 1988.

Corbett, Jim. *The Man-Eaters of Kumaon*. New York: Oxford UP, 1946.

Das, Manoj. *Books Forever*. New Delhi: National Book Trust, 1973.

Edgerton, Franklin, trans. and interpreter. *The Bhagavad Gita*. New York: Harper, 1964.

Khorana, Meena. "The River Is Eternal: Nature Mysticism and Vedanta Philosophy in Ruskin Bond's *Angry River*." *The Lion and the Unicorn* 19.2 (Dec. 1995): 253–68.

Krishnaleela: A Childhood Story of Lord Krishna. Faridabad: Thomson, 1977.

Mehra, G. N. *Bhutan: Land of the Peaceful Dragon*. New Delhi: Vikas, 1974.

Menon, Navin. "Children's Literature in India: The Changing Trends." *Telling Tales: Children's Literature in India*. Ed. Amit Dasgupta. New Delhi: Indian Council for Cultural Relations and New Age International Publishers, 1995. 53–66.

Nikhilananda, Swami, trans. and ed. *The Upanishads*. Abridged ed. New York and Evanston: Harper, 1964.

Rose, Deborah Lee. *The People Who Hugged Trees: An Environmental Folktale*. Niwot, CO: Roberts Rinehart, 1990. End page.

Saraiya, Indu. "A Place in the Shade." *Independent* [Bombay] 10 Dec. 1989: III.

8

The Mountains Are Kind to Writers

The late 1980s and 1990s brought a great measure of success to Ruskin Bond as a writer for children and adults. He always had attracted loyal readers and publishers in India and abroad, but now public recognition was again given to his work. Not since 1957, when the John Llewellyn Rhys Memorial Prize was awarded to his first novel, *The Room on the Roof*, had he won a major award. He received three highly prestigious national awards in India: in 1987, the Indian Council for Child Education Award for his "pivotal role in the development of children's literature in India"; the 1992 Sahitya Akademi Award for English Writing in India for *Our Trees Still Grow in Dehra*; and in 1999, the Padma Shri, awarded by the president of India to an outstanding Indian citizen. In 1996 and 1998, he was nominated, by the Association of Writers and Illustrators for Children, as India's candidate for the Hans Christian Andersen Author Award, given biannually by the International Board on Books for Young People for lifetime achievement as an author of books for children and young adults. The international jury declared him one of the five author finalists in 1998. In 1995 his children's book *Binya's Blue Umbrella* was judged one of the year's Ten Best Books by *Parenting Magazine* and it received the Reading Magic Award for "distinguished achievement in children's literature." Another children's book, *Getting Granny's Glasses*, was short-listed for the Carnegie Medal when it was first published in the United Kingdom.

This public acclaim has coincided with the coming-of-age of publishing in India. Now more than fifty years after Independence, the Indian publishing industry is experiencing phenomenal growth, making publishing more economically viable for both writers and publishers. According to a report in *Asian/Pacific Book Development* (*ABD*) magazine, "Besides the United States and UK, India has the largest volume of English language publication and is among the 12 largest book publishing countries in the production of titles. Again, India is the largest book producer in the third world with around 40,000 titles being brought out by an estimated 8,000 publishers in English and various Indian languages" ("Publishing Circumstances" 12–13). While only 2 percent of the population is English-speaking, with a total population of over 1 billion, that figure constitutes a sizable readership. In addition, the English-speaking population mostly belongs to the upper- and upper-middle class and hence can afford to purchase books. With this strong base of readers in English, Bond's audience has definitely shifted from readers abroad to readers in India.

Bond's writing career of over fifty years spans the development of the publishing industry in India, from the time when "it was still in the womb" (T. Singh 115), when writing for magazines or publishing abroad were the only outlets for authors in English, to the current vigorous publishing atmosphere. Likewise, when Bond first started to publish in 1951, Indian writing in English was called Indo-Anglian Literature, emphasizing the colonial connection of the language and/or the literary influence on the writers. Today, writer Shashi Tharoor makes a passionate argument in favor of the more accurate term, Indian Writing in English, because it acknowledges that English writing is one of the national literatures of India ("Expanding"). In the last two decades, Indian authors in English—such as Anita Desai, Jhumpa Lahiri, V. S. Naipaul, Arundhati Roy, Bharati Mukherjee, Salman Rushdie, and Vikram Seth—have won the most prestigious international awards for fiction. Bond does not as yet have the same stature abroad for his adult writing, but he is highly regarded as a children's author. He has published over twenty children's titles in the United Kingdom and the United States (some in both countries), and some of his most popular works—such as *Angry River*, *The Blue Umbrella*, *Grandfather's Private Zoo,* and *Tigers Forever*—have also been published in Dutch, French, Spanish, German, and Danish translations. In India, Bond has been a pioneer in the field of children's and young adult literature and has made an outstanding contribution to the modern short story. With characteristic modesty, he writes:

> Among writers, I am not one of the big guns. I am not even a little gun. I'm just a pebble lying on the beach. But I like to think that I'm a smooth, round, colourful pebble, and that someone will pick me up, derive a little pleasure from holding me, and possibly even put me in his, or her, pocket. (Introduction, *Lamp* xi)

While Bond has remained popular with Indian readers ranging from children and young adults to adults and the elderly, prior to the 1990s he was virtually ignored by the Indian literary academy as someone who wrote for newspapers and magazines, or who was "only" a children's author or a regional writer for adults. Any survey of Indian writing in English is incomplete without an in-depth discussion of Bond's works because, over a long writing career, he has published many novels, short stories, poems, and essays that have withstood the test of time. He is a versatile, original, and elegant writer who handles a variety of genres and themes with equal grace and skill. Prabhat K. Singh's full-length study, *The Creative Contours of Ruskin Bond: An Anthology of Critical Writings*, has filled this void in Indian scholarship. In the preface, Singh states: it is a "'quirk of irony' that the winner of [the] John Llewellyn Rhys Memorial Prize (London) in 1957...did not catch the attention of Indian readers and critics as extensively as he deserved until the Sahitya Akademi honoured him with a national award for literature...in 1992," while many "inferior talents have come in focus chiefly because they chose to write on popular and somewhat sensational subjects like apartheid or woman's lib, religio-communal frenzy or socio-political strife" (x).

Bond's work has been foundational in the development of young adult and children's literature in India. His books especially fill a void in young adult reading, because many adolescent novels, far from exploring the inner person, are limited to mystery and adventure stories, school stories, and novels of progress. Bond has refrained from the postcolonial fad of writing the formulaic Enid Blyton-style mysteries and adventures that are so popular in India. He places great importance on good books for young readers, and his stories express empathy for children, respect for their intelligence, and faith in their ability to shape the future. He enjoys writing for children and being with his young readers. Although shy and reserved by nature, when in the midst of children he can enthrall a large audience with jokes about his name "Bond," give advice on how to nurture their writing skills, and answer their many questions. The launching of each new book or visit to a school is attended by overwhelming crowds of children eager to get his autograph or to talk to him. Bond is equally helpful to adult writers for children. In 2001 a group of approximately twenty writers met in a writer's workshop in Landour to talk with the author, create, and discuss their work. A year later the result of this weekend celebration of writers was a Festschrift of short stories about adolescence, dedicated to Bond: *Days of Innocence: Stories for Ruskin Bond.*

Bond has also contributed to making three generations of Indian school children into readers. His short stories, poems, and essays—even those written forty or fifty years back—are widely anthologized in school texts, and his books are required reading in many schools throughout the country where English is the medium of instruction. Students' Stores, an educational publisher based in New Delhi, has used several Bond titles in its series of graded readers, divided according to four levels of difficulty, for students of English as a second language. *An Island of Trees* and *Tigers Forever* are being used as supplementary readers in progressive schools, not just because they offer good samples of prose writing but because they touch the young reader in a very personal way. His works have been translated into twelve major Indian languages including Hindi, Bengali, Assamese, Gujarati, Tamil, Punjabi, and Malayalam.

Bond's stories have also become part of popular culture. *A Flight of Pigeons* was made into a major Hindi motion picture, *Junoon*, which won the President's Award in 1979, directed by Shyam Benegal, and starring the famous actor Shashi Kapoor in the leading role. Bond's deftness at creating believable characters with whom young readers can readily identify has also resulted in a thirteen-episode television serial, *Ek tha Rusty* (Once there was Rusty), which was produced by Shubhadarshini Singh and aired on the Doordarshan television channel in 1996. Thirteen additional episodes are in the planning stage.

Bond's popularity as a writer is evidenced by the rapidity with which his novels, short stories, poems, and essays are being reprinted in collections. In the 1990s alone, he published fifteen collections by various publishers in India: three volumes of autobiographical writings, including memoirs, essays, and extracts from diaries and journals; two nonfiction books and travel pieces on Mussoorie and the Garhwal region; his two adolescent novels republished in a single book; two omnibus volumes of all his published fiction for children and adults; three collections of short fiction for a general audience with a thematic focus—on animal stories, nature stories, and ghost stories; a book containing two novellas for adults; and three volumes of short stories on

Indian Railways, ghost stories, and love stories that he both edited and contributed to. This list does not include the many books for children published in India and abroad. In addition, each year he has regularly published stories and essays in a variety of English-language newspapers and magazines such as *Cricket* (Peru, IL), *Highlights for Children* (Honesdale, PA), *The Christian Science Monitor* (Boston), and *School Magazine* (Sydney). His stories are also included in a variety of anthologies such as *Young Oxford Book of Ghost Stories*, *Six Inches to England and Other Childlike Views of Our World: An Anthology of International Children's Stories*, *Young Oxford Book of Train Stories*, and *Nasty Endings—I*. Marianne Carus, founder and editor-in-chief of *Cricket*, says that she has admired Bond's work since 1974, when he first started publishing with her: "Our *Cricket* readers enjoyed Ruskin's stories just as much as my staff and I did. Ruskin had a delicious sense of humor, and knew how to hold a child's attention."

In the new millennium, he has already published a new edition of his out-of-print collection of poems for children, a collection of thirty-seven stories for children, two collections of short stories for a general audience, and another autobiographical volume, entitled *Landour Days: A Writer's Journal*. Penguin Books India is bringing out a two-volume series of all his "Rusty" stories, tracing the development of Bond's autobiographical character, Rusty, from childhood in Jamnagar to adolescence in Dehra. Included in the set are such stories as *The Hidden Pool* and "Escape from Java," where the protagonist is not specifically Rusty. The first volume, *Rusty: The Boy from the Hills*, will be released in 2002, and the second, *More Tales of Rusty: The Boy from the Hills*, in 2003. Thus, Bond's short stories and essays published from the 1950s onward have become available in book form for a second and third generation of readers. In several instances, he has revised, enhanced, or combined two stories into a longer piece for these collections. Some collections—such as *Panther's Moon and Other Stories*—have gone into several reprints. According to David Davidar, CEO of Penguin Books India, Bond's main publisher in India, Ruskin Bond is "certainly one of the big guns in the writer's pantheon" (4).

> There are adult books and children's novels, travelogues and essays, poems and anthologies, biographical sketches and memoirs, all bearing the distinctive Bond style, deep yet uncluttered, evocative yet spare, gentle yet searching and still the writing flows as strong and as vibrant as it has ever been and that is something we continue to be grateful for. (Davidar 4)

With the improved publishing environment in India—and with increasing financial security for Bond—a new phase in Bond's already successful career as a writer is developing. Although he will continue writing for children, Bond has started a longer project: he is working on a historical romance about Frederic "Pahari" Wilson, the romantic adventurer who came to Garhwal in the 1850s and became a part of local legend.

In spite of the difference in time, Bond is frequently compared to Rudyard Kipling, perhaps because both are Anglo-Indian writers who are fascinated with ghost stories and jungle lore. While Bond shares Kipling's love for India and admires his skill in capturing the essence of the Himalayas and bringing the Indian scene to life, he does not subscribe to Kipling's colonial stance of superiority and the "White man's burden" (see "The Man"). Like Kipling, Bond observes urban society with amusement and mild satire, but unlike Kipling he also directs his ironic gaze at the racial prejudice of the British, as he does in "Calypso Christmas." Bond states that "Kipling saw India from a Britisher's eye. He romanticised about India but could not accept her as she was. But then he did not stay long enough to know India" (qtd. in Kapoor et al.).

Is the comparison with Kipling made because Bond is regarded as speaking from within a Eurocentric perspective? Does Indian scholar Harish Trivedi's criticism that Indian writers in English are "cut off from the experiential mainstream and from that common cultural matrix...shared with writers of all other Indian languages" apply to Bond? (qtd. in Tharoor). Bond knows India as an insider. He writes with authenticity and emotional engagement of the Garhwal Himalayas that have shaped his personality and worldview. While Kipling left India and went on to write about other subjects, Bond experienced a sense of exile away from India and returned to live permanently in the country that he loved and considered home. "My reality was India," he writes in the introduction to *When Darkness Falls and Other Stories*, "and I needed more of India and less of England for my literary aspirations to be satisfied" (ix). His living in Mussoorie is significant because the town is a blend of British and Indian history, culture, and legends. He has synthesized his Anglo-Indian heritage with the indigenous culture, languages, and ethos of the Garhwal region. However, Bond does not assume the hyphenated identity of "Anglo-Indian" and prefers to call himself "just Indian." His unique contribution to postcolonial, post-Independence literature is this hybridity, this dual vision that infuses complexity and richness into his writing. Author Mulk Raj Anand put it eloquently when he stated that Bond's "novels and stories seem to have emerged from within Indian homes" (34).

The short fiction genre is ideally suited to the author's temperament and emotional response to the subjects he cares about. He likes the unified structure and format of the short story or novella, because "[i]t finishes soon, in the intensity of the mood and feeling" (qtd. in Kapoor et al.). Yet, this brevity should not be mistaken for a lack of depth or an inability to explore complex issues. His meticulously structured plots turn on a single event that either catches the protagonist in a revealing situation or enables him to resolve a personal dilemma. Bond's skillful artistry then juxtaposes these individual dramas against larger social, moral, or metaphysical issues. One theme that his stories repeatedly explore is the upheaval often caused by the city encroaching into or exploiting the village or small town. He develops the trope of the small town versus the big city into an aesthetic principle that is reminiscent of the pastoral tradition in literature. The small town or rural Himalayan setting is a place that endures, changes slowly, and is equated with purity and contemplation. In contrast, the city has lost its connection with the land and its inhabitants have become aggressive and materialistic at the expense of basic human values. This longing for a time gone by also creates a tension between past and present. However, Bond's stories are not just nostalgic or romantic relics of the past, because the past is a living presence in the lives of his protagonists and the small town.

Bond declares that his life both as a writer and as a person "are one and the same thing. I live through my writing, just as my writing lives through me" (Introduction, *Lamp* x). Over the decades, he has maintained his autobiographical style of writing, using his personal experiences and observations as the source for the plots, characters, and settings of his stories. "I'm not very inventive where plots are concerned," says Bond, "I get ideas from what I've known and am familiar with" (qtd. in Dhir). However, he does invent for narrative expediency and, with a few exceptions, his children's books are mostly objective, based on the lives of the children from the nearby hills. But the whole is projected so convincingly that the reader takes it as pure autobiography because Bond establishes an intimate relationship through the first person singular. "The 'I' takes one in immediate confidence so that no doubt arises as to the authenticity or credibility of the narratives" (Haider 126). The distinctions between the writer and his characters seem irrelevant as the stories explore the pleasures of childhood, the loneliness and pain of unrequited love, the satisfaction of knowing that the old tiger has escaped the hunters, or a subliminal acceptance of the duality of nature. What is important is that Bond strongly draws readers into the experience. Diana Athill has this to say about his approach:

> Your snag is, surely, that you are a writer who works best from very close to your own experience—which means that one is terribly dependent on the nature of one's experience. Only so much that is of general validity happens to one—and only so much of what happens to one strikes down to the level from which one writes. I sometimes feel very envious of people with the other kind of mind, full of invention. But I still like best the kind of writing which goes inwards rather than outwards.

In seeking inspiration from his personal experiences, Bond is perhaps limiting the range of his subject matter. But, as he says in the introduction to *The Night Train at Deoli and Other Stories*, "I can't really write unless I am in love with my subject" (no pag.). He "cannot breathe life into" political leaders, media tycoons, or businessmen, because "one has to peel off too many layers of protective armour to get at the flesh and blood that lies beneath the skin" (*Lamp* 196). He writes for a special type of "gentle reader" who is interested in the beauty of nature and the dignity in the lives of ordinary people rather than in stormy events. While he does not write provocative social protest stories, his stories deal with social issues such as preservation of the Himalayan environment, rights of animals, respect for humanity, and a sense of justice and fair play. Momentous events do take place in his stories—the building of a mountain road that destroys trees and displaces wildlife, a solitary tree on the hillside that saves the life of a truck driver and his crew, and the concerns of a hill boy who cannot go to school because a man-eater is at large. There is a universal quality to his writing that transcends the regional locale and the autobiographical element—that is, the human endeavor to survive against odds and to preserve what is beautiful and meaningful.

Bond's deep and abiding love for nature, his affection for his characters, simple approach to living, and mild and gentle manners find resonance in his seemingly effortless style. The charm of his writing rests in the ease with which his graceful prose gently directs readers to contemplate both universal truths as well as a thoughtful exploration of questions that perplex his characters. Most see him as a Romantic, a nature writer, but he is also a humorist who loves to poke fun at human folly and expose hypocrisy and immoral behavior, especially in people who are in positions of power. His prose is in turn lyrical, sensuous, whimsical, sentimental, satirical, and thought provoking—and Bond works hard to achieve this effect. He calls himself a "wordsmith": "I have tried to use words creatively and lovingly. The gift of putting together words and sentences to make stories or poems or essays has carried me through life with a certain serenity and inner harmony which could not have come from an unloved vocation" (*Lamp* 193).

Bond's writing crosses barriers: descriptive details, telling statements, characters, events, and themes recur in a variety of contexts throughout his oeuvre. For example, images of tendrils creeping towards Rusty's father or grandfather, the shadow of an ancient tree on the house, and a bougainvillea branch peeping in through the open window; and statements like "The monsoon was going to break that day. I knew it, the birds knew it, the grass knew it" ("Sensualist" 116) appear as a refrain in many of his stories and essays. Likewise, the same characters reappear like old acquaintances. Dukhi, the gardener in the old palace in Jamnagar, is also featured in the Rusty stories set in Dehra, and again when the adult protagonist visits Shamli—always full of sage advice and in tune with nature. His name may change in some stories, but we recognize him nevertheless. Such repetition lends rhythm, cohesiveness, and continuity to Bond's work.

Over the years, Bond has maintained his integrity as a writer and has worked toward his goals and vision with single-minded devotion. His greatest achievement is that he persevered in his dream of becoming a full-time writer. The philosophy that motivated and sustained him is articulated by the old, double-bent beggar in the essay "What's Your Dream?": "You must work for your dream, and move towards it all the time, and discard all those things that come in the way of finding it, and then, if you don't expect too much too quickly, you'll find your freedom, your room of your own" (23). Bond has stayed focused on his dream, and even after having achieved it, he does not want to lose it all by becoming "greedy, or careless, and start taking everything for granted" (23). Success and recognition have not corrupted him, and he continues to live a simple life—"unhurried, even-paced, sensual, in step with the natural world, most at home with humble people" (*Rain* 246).

WORKS CITED

Anand, Mulk Raj. "Ruskin Bond." P. K. Singh, *Creative Contours* 33–35.

Athill, Diana. Letter to Ruskin Bond, 23 Mar. 1964. Qtd. in *Scenes from a Writer's Life: A Memoir*. By Ruskin Bond. New Delhi: Penguin, 1997. Front fly leaf.

Bond, Ruskin. *The Blue Umbrella. Six Inches to England and Other Childlike Views of Our World: An Anthology of International Children's Stories*. Ed. Margaret Robinson Millar. Compiled by Jeannie Ferver. Alton, NH: Andover Green, 2001. 19–40.

___. "Calypso Christmas." *Collected Fiction*. By Bond. New Delhi: Penguin, 1999. 457–60.

___. "Face in the Night." *Nasty Endings—I*. Ed. Dennis Pepper. Oxford: Oxford UP, 1997. 43–45.

___. Introduction. Bond, *Lamp* ix–xiii.

___. *The Lamp Is Lit: Leaves from a Journal*. New Delhi: Penguin, 1998.

___. *Landour Days: A Writer's Journal*. New Delhi: Penguin, 2002.

___. "The Man Who Was Kipling." Bond, *Night Train* 31–33.

___. *The Night Train at Deoli and Other Stories*. New Delhi: Penguin, 1988.

___. *Rain in the Mountains: Notes from the Himalayas*. New Delhi: Viking/Penguin, 1993.

___. "The Sensualist: A Cautionary Tale." *Strangers in the Night: Two Novellas*. By Bond. New Delhi: Penguin, 1996. 81–143.

___. "Topaz." *Young Oxford Book of Ghost Stories*. Ed. Dennis Pepper. Oxford: Oxford UP, 1999. 20–25.

___. "The Tunnel." *Young Oxford Book of Train Stories*. Ed. Dennis Hamley. Oxford: Oxford UP, 2001. 21–28.

___. "What's Your Dream?" *A Garland of Memories*. By Bond. New Delhi: Mukul Prakashan, 1982. 22–24.

___. *When Darkness Falls and Other Stories*. New Delhi: Penguin, 2001.

Carus, Marianne. Letter to Meena Khorana, 1 April 2002.

Davidar, David. "Ruskin Bond: The Man with the Golden Pen." *Books Today* (April–June 2000): 4.

Days of Innocence: Stories for Ruskin Bond. New Delhi: Namita Gokhale/Roli, 2002.

Dhir, Aruna. "'I Haven't Done All That I Could Have…'" Review Section, *The Sunday Times of India* [New Delhi] 14 Feb. 1993: 6.

Haider, Aijaz. "The Woman in Bond's Short Stories." P. K. Singh, *Creative Contours* 125–31.

Kapoor, Divyaksh, Ritu Chopra, and Deepti Dar. "Committed to Writing." The Times Offspring Section, *The Times of India* [New Delhi] 19 March 1990.

"Publishing Circumstances." *Asian/Pacific Book Development (ABD)* 32.2 (2001): 12–16.

Singh, Prabhat K., ed. *The Creative Contours of Ruskin Bond: An Anthology of Critical Writings*. New Delhi: Pencraft, 1995.

Singh, Tejeshwar. "Publishing in India: Crisis and Opportunity." *Publishing in the Third World: Knowledge and Development*. Eds. Philip G. Altbach, Amadio A. Arboleda, and S. Gopinathan. Portsmouth, NH: Heinemann, 1985. 111–30.

Tharoor, Shashi. "Expanding Boundaries with a Colonial Legacy." Website: <www.nytimes.com/2001/07/30/books/30THAR>.

Selected Bibliography

RUSKIN BOND'S BOOKS FOR ADULTS

Autobiographical Works

The Lamp Is Lit: Leaves from a Journal. New Delhi: Penguin, 1998.
Landour Days: A Writer's Journal. New Delhi: Penguin, 2002.
Rain in the Mountains: Notes from the Himalayas. New Delhi: Viking/Penguin, 1993.
Scenes from a Writer's Life: A Memoir. New Delhi: Penguin, 1997.

Poetry

It Isn't Time That's Passing: Poems 1970–1971. Calcutta: Writers Workshop, 1972.
Lone Fox Dancing: Lyric Poems. Calcutta: Writers Workshop, 1975.

Nonfiction

Beautiful Garhwal. Dehra Dun: English Book Depot, 1988.
Ganga Descends. Illus. M. Chakraborty; with charcoal illus. from *Gazetteer.* Dehra Dun: English Book Depot, 1992.
Garhwal: Heaven in Himalayas. With color photographs. Dehra Dun: English Book Depot, circa 1988.
A Garland of Memories. New Delhi: Mukul Prakashan, 1982.
Mussoorie and Landour: Days of Wine and Roses. Illus. Ganesh Saili. New Delhi: Lustre, 1992.
Strange Men, Strange Places. Bombay: Pearl, 1969. New Delhi: Rupa, 1992.

Novels

An Axe for the Rani. Delhi: Hind Pocket Books, 1972.
A Flight of Pigeons. Bombay: India Book House, 1980. New Delhi: Penguin, 2002.
Love Is a Sad Song. New Delhi: Orient Paperbacks, 1975.

Collections

Complete Short Stories and Novels. New Delhi: Viking/Penguin, 1996. As *Collected Fiction.* New Delhi: Penguin, 1999.
Delhi Is Not Far: The Best of Ruskin Bond. New Delhi: Penguin, 1994.
Friends in Small Places: Ruskin Bond's Unforgettable People. New Delhi: Penguin, 2000.
Ghosts of a Hill Station. Bombay: India Book House, 1983.
A Girl from Copenhagen. New Delhi: India Paperbacks, 1977.
The Man-Eater of Manjari. New Delhi: Sterling, 1974.
My First Love and Other Stories. Bombay: Pearl, 1968.
The Neighbour's Wife and Other Stories. Madras: Higginbothams, 1965, 1967.
The Night Train at Deoli and Other Stories. New Delhi: Penguin, 1988.
Our Trees Still Grow in Dehra. New Delhi: Penguin, 1991.
Strangers in the Night: Two Novellas. New Delhi: Penguin, 1996. In Hindi as *Raat ke Ajnabi: Do Laghu Upanyasa.* Trans. Prabhat K. Singh. New Delhi: Atmaram, 1998.
Time Stops at Shamli and Other Stories. New Delhi: Penguin, 1989.
When Darkness Falls and Other Stories. New Delhi: Penguin, 2001.

Edited Works

The Penguin Book of Classical Indian Love Stories and Lyrics. New Delhi: Penguin, 1996.
The Penguin Book of Indian Ghost Stories. New Delhi: Penguin, 1993.
The Penguin Book of Indian Railway Stories. New Delhi: Penguin, 1994.
Ruskin Bond's Green Book. New Delhi: Roli, 1995.

RUSKIN BOND'S BOOKS FOR YOUNG ADULTS

Fiction

Panther's Moon and Other Stories. Illus. Suddhasattwa Basu. New Delhi: Puffin, 1991.
The Room on the Roof. London: André Deutsch, 1956. New York: Coward McCann, 1957. New Delhi: Students' Stores, 1981. New Delhi: Penguin, 1987. Jointly with *Vagrants in the Valley* as *"The Room on the Roof" and*

"Vagrants in the Valley": Two Novels of Adolescence. New Delhi: Penguin, 1993. In German as *Die Strasse zum Bazar*. Munich: Albert Langen–Georg Müller [1957]. Book Club ed. Illus. with line drawings. Hamburg: Deutsche Hausbücherei [1957].

A Season of Ghosts. New Delhi: Viking, 1999.

The Young Vagrants. Bombay: India Book House, 1981. As *Vagrants in the Valley*, jointly with *The Room on the Roof* as *"The Room on the Roof" and "Vagrants in the Valley": Two Novels of Adolescence*. New Delhi: Penguin, 1993.

RUSKIN BOND'S BOOKS FOR CHILDREN

Poetry

Granny's Tree Climbing and Other Poems. Illus. Tapas Guha. Gurgaon: Scholastic, 2000.

To Live in Magic: A Book of Nature Poems. Illus. Suddhasattwa Basu. New Delhi: Thomson, 1985.

Nonfiction

The Last Tiger. New Delhi: Publications Division, Government of India, 1971.

Man of Destiny: A Biography of Jawaharlal Nehru. New Delhi: Orient Paperbacks, 1976.

Who's Who at the Zoo. Illus. Raghu Rai. New Delhi: National Book Trust, 1974.

The Wonderful World of Insects, Trees and Wild Flowers. Illus. Kamal Kishore. Bombay: India Book House, 1968.

The World of Trees. Illus. Siddhartha Banerjee. New Delhi: National Book Trust, 1974.

Traditional Stories

The Adventures of Rama and Sita. Illus. Valerie Littlewood. London: Julia MacRae, 1987.

Hanuman to the Rescue. Cover illus. Uday Shankar. New Delhi: Rupa, 1993.

Tales and Legends from India. Illus. Sally Scott. London: Julia MacRae, 1982. Illus. Scott. New Delhi: Rupa, 1990.

Tales Told at Twilight. Illus. Madhu Powle. Bombay: India Book House, 1970.

Fiction

The Adventures of Rusty. Illus. Imtiaz Dharker. New Delhi: Thomson, 1981. New Delhi: Students' Stores, 1991.

Angry River. Illus. Trevor Stubley. London: Hamish Hamilton, 1972. Illus. Stubley. New Delhi: Rupa, 1992. In French as *Sita et la rivière*. Paris: Rageot, 1977. In Dutch as *De grote overstroming*. Trans. Els van Delden. Illus. Frank der Horst. Tilburg: Zwijsen, 1988.

Big Business. Illus. Valerie Littlewood. London: Hamish Hamilton, 1979. Illus. Littlewood. New Delhi: Students' Stores, 1987.

The Blue Umbrella. Illus. Trevor Stubley. London: Hamish Hamilton, 1974. New Delhi: Students' Stores, 1986. Illus. Stubley. Calcutta: Rupa, 1992. As *Binya's Blue Umbrella*. Illus. Vera Rosenberry. Honesdale, PA: Boyds Mills, 1995. In French as *Une ombrelle bleu-rêve*. Trans. Caroline Nyro. Illus. Dominique Goupil. Paris: Rageot, 1978. In Dutch as *Bleu Parasol*. Kosmos, 1978.

The Cherry Tree. Illus. Valerie Littlewood. London: Hamish Hamilton, 1980. New Delhi: Frank, 1994. As *Cherry Tree*. Illus. Allan Eitzen. Honesdale, PA: Caroline House, 1991.

Cricket for the Crocodile. Illus. Barbara Walker. London: Julia MacRae, 1986.

Dust on the Mountain. Illus. Nigel Murray. London: Julia MacRae, 1990.

Earthquake. Illus. Valerie Littlewood. London: Julia MacRae, 1984.

The Eyes of the Eagle. Illus. Valerie Littlewood. London: Julia MacRae, 1987.

Flames in the Forest. Illus. Valerie Littlewood. London: Julia MacRae, 1981.

Getting Granny's Glasses. Illus. Barbara Walker. London: Julia MacRae, 1985. New Delhi: Frank, 1996.

Ghost Trouble. Illus. Barbara Walker. London: Julia MacRae, 1989. In Danish as *Et venligt spøelse*. [N. place]: Munksgaard, 1991.

The Hidden Pool. Illus. Arup Das. New Delhi: Children's Book Trust, 1966. New Delhi: Students' Stores, 1987.

Leopard on the Mountain. Cambridge, Engl.: Cambridge UP, 1998.

Night of the Leopard. Illus. Eileen Green. London: Hamish Hamilton, 1979. New Delhi: Students' Stores, 1986.

Once upon a Monsoon Time. Hyderabad: Orient Longman, 1974. In German as *Damals zur Zeit des Monsuns*. Illus. Ingrid Hegemann. Recklinghausen: Georg Bitter, 1985.

Panther's Moon. Illus. Tom Feelings. New York: Random House, 1969.

Quakes and Flames. Illus. Subir Roy. New Delhi: National Book Trust, 1994.

Snake Trouble. Illus. Barbara Walker. London: Julia MacRae, 1990.

Tiger Roars, Eagle Soars. London: Walker, 1994.

Tigers Forever. Illus. Valerie Littlewood. London: Julia MacRae, 1983. New York: Watts, 1983. In Danish as *Den sidste tiger*. Illus. Littlewood. [N. place]: Munksgaard, 1987.

Collections

A Bond with the Mountains: Stories, Thoughts and Poems. Illus. Tapas Guha. New Delhi: Ratna Sagar, 1998.

The Eyes of the Eagle and Other Stories. New Delhi: Students' Stores, 1990.

Grandfather's Private Zoo. Illus. Mario Miranda. Bombay: India Book House, 1967. New Delhi: Students' Stores, 1992. In Dutch as *Een huis vol dieren.* Trans. Els Pelgrom. Illus. Mario. Amsterdam: Bert Bakker, 1984.

An Island of Trees: Nature Stories and Poems. Illus. Suddhasattwa Basu. Delhi: Ratna Sagar, 1992.

The Road to the Bazaar. Illus. Valerie Littlewood. London: Julia MacRae, 1980. Rev. and exp. ed. Illus. Littlewood. London: Julia MacRae, 1991. Illus. Littlewood. New Delhi: Rupa, 1993, 1997. In Spanish as *El camino del bazar.* Trans. Teodoro Larriba. Illus. Littlewood. Madrid: Ediciones SM, 1982.

The Ruskin Bond Children's Omnibus. New Delhi: Rupa, 1995.

Ruskin Bond's Treasury of Stories for Children. Illus. Tapas Guha. New Delhi: Viking, 2000.

Three Short Stories in Cricket. New Delhi: Students' Stores, 1990.

Tigers Forever: Stories and Poems. Illus. Tapas Guha. New Delhi: Ratna Sagar, 1996.

FORTHCOMING TITLES

Bangalore—Along the Fairway: A History of the Bangalore Golf Club. Bangalore: Bangalore Golf Club.

Ghost Stories of the Raj. Ed. Ruskin Bond. New Delhi: Rupa.

More Tales of Rusty: The Boy from the Hills. New Delhi: Penguin.

Rusty: The Boy from the Hills. New Delhi: Penguin.

CRITICAL WORKS ON RUSKIN BOND

The Hans Christian Andersen Nominees Special. *Writer and Illustrator* 17.4 (July–Sept. 1998): 1–32.

Singh, Prabhat K., ed. *The Creative Contours of Ruskin Bond: An Anthology of Critical Writings.* New Delhi: Pencraft, 1995.

DISSERTATIONS ON RUSKIN BOND

Basu, Sutapa. "Ruskin Bond: The Autobiographical Element in His Fiction." Diss. Chaudhri Charan Singh University (Meerut), in progress.

Dobhal, Brahma Nand. "Treatment of Humanism in the Works of Ruskin Bond." D. Phil. diss. Garhwal University (Srinagar, Garhwal), submitted.

Nayak, Felix. "The Fiction of Ruskin Bond: A Critical Study." Diss. Ravishanker University (Raipur), in progress.

Taqui, Ishrat G. "The Short Stories of Ruskin Bond: A Thematic Study." M. Phil. diss. University of Bombay (Vidyanagari), 1991.

RUSKIN BOND WEBSITE

<http://www.ruskinbond.com>.

SPECIAL COLLECTIONS

Ruskin Bond's diaries, photographs, letters, manuscripts, holographs, and other papers have been acquired by the Department of Special Collections, Mugar Memorial Library, Boston University, Boston.

Index

About the Author

MEENA G. KHORANA is Professor of English at Morgan State University. She is the author of *The Indian Subcontinent in Literature for Children and Young Adults* (Greenwood, 1991) and *Africa in Literature for Children and Young Adults* (Greenwood, 1994).